PINKERTON
America's First Private Eye

Allan Pinkerton

PINKERTON
America's First Private Eye

By

Richard Wormser

WALKER AND COMPANY   NEW YORK

First published in the United States of America in 1990
by Walker Publishing Company, Inc.

Published simultaneously in Canada by Thomas Allen & Son
Canada, Limited, Markham, Onatario

Library of Congress Cataloging-in-Publication Data

Wormser, Richard
Pinkerton : America's first private eye / written by Richard Wormser.
Summary: Examines the life of the detective who founded his own
agency and introduced a system of recording criminals to help track
them down and tie them to crimes.
ISBN 0-8027-6964-0. — ISBN 0-8027-6965-9 (lib. bdg.)
1. Pinkerton, Allan, 1819–1884 — Juvenile literature.
2. Detectives — United States — Biography — Juvenile literature.
[1. Pinkerton, Allan, 1819–1884. 2. Detectives.] I. Title.
HV7911.P4675W67   1990
363.2′89′092 — dc20   [B]   [92]   90-12362

Printed in the United States of America

2   4   6   8   10   9   7   5   3   1

To Annie, for everything.

Acknowledgments

The photographs and illustrations reproduced in this book are all taken from the public domain, with the exception of the picture of Robert and William on page 111. For permission to reprint that picture we thank the Chicago Historical Society, Chicago, Illinois.

The author would like to thank the following organizations for supplying pictures and drawings, and for assisting with the research necessary to write this book.

Pinkerton Security and Investigation Services
The Chicago Historical Society
The New York Public Library
The National Archives
The Library of Congress
History Works, Inc.

CONTENTS

1

Peaceably if We Can, Forcibly if We Must

———————— 👁 ————————

Allan Pinkerton, America's first "private eye," was a man of many contradictions. He was a conservative radically opposed to slavery, a cautious man who risked his life pursuing criminals, a militant labor organizer who suppressed the labor movement, a domestic tyrant who championed a woman's right to be a detective. To some he was a superhero; to others a villain. But even his enemies conceded he was the best private detective of his time.

During his twenty-eight year career, Allan Pinkerton and his agents investigated over a thousand crimes. They solved murders and robberies, hunted outlaws, exposed con-men and broke up counterfeiting rings. Pinkerton investigated cases in a manner worthy of Sherlock Holmes. He followed every lead, analyzed every clue, took nothing for granted, and made keen deductions based on the evidence he gathered. Some of his most successful cases were solved because he noticed the way a picture hung on a wall, discovered a charred piece of cloth in a fireplace, or overheard a chance remark by a stranger. He single-handedly built a detective agency that was the nineteenth-century equivalent of the FBI. He organized the best criminal identification system of its time using photographs and the personal histories of thousands of known criminals. His agency's motto, "The Eye That Never Sleeps," was the source of the expression "private eye."

If Allan Pinkerton had just been a private detective solving cases, he might have been forgotten by history. But Pinkerton was involved in many of the exciting dramas of the nineteenth century. He was a fighter in the great struggle against slavery and he organized America's first secret service during the Civil War. Pinkerton chased famous outlaws such as Jesse James and created an industrial police force that was used during the labor movement's bitter struggle to organize.

Allan Pinkerton began life in a world filled with crime. He was born on August 25, 1819, in a slum section of Glasgow, Scotland, known as the Gorbals. His parents, William and Isabell Pinkerton, had four sons, but two of Allan's brothers died young. Allan's father had been married before, but his first wife died, leaving seven children behind. Allan later said that his stepbrothers and stepsisters did not get along with his father and all left home while he was still a small child.

The Gorbals was one of the worst slums of nineteenth-century Europe. A visitor to the city at that time wrote: "I have seen human degradation in some of the worst places but I can say

The house in the Gorbals where Allan Pinkerton was born.

that I did not believe, until I visited Glasgow, that so large an amount of filth, crime, misery, and disease existed in one spot in any civilized country."

It was a small miracle that Allan and his brother Robert survived childhood. The mortality rate for children in the Gorbals was staggering. Four out of every ten children died before the age of five. Thousands were victims of the cholera and typhus epidemics that periodically ravaged the city. Disease was rampant because there was little or no sanitation. Waste was deposited in open sewers. Dung heaps were piled up in the courtyards of buildings. Streets and lanes were narrow, twisting, dark, and dirty with little fresh air. Many houses were more than two-hundred-years old and infested with rats and roaches. In some buildings as many as twenty people were packed into a single room.

As a child, Allan must have constantly seen domestic and criminal violence. Drunkenness, homelessness, wife-beating, and child abuse were common in the Gorbals. Murders and robberies were reported in the newspapers daily. There were dark rumors that bodysnatchers lurked in the doorways with chloroform-soaked rags, waiting to knock their victims out, then rob and murder them, and sell their bodies to medical schools.

Poverty caused by massive unemployment was the major reason for crime in the Gorbals. In the early part of the nineteenth-century, Glasgow had become the foremost industrial city of Scotland. Tens of thousands of people worked in spinning mills, textile factories, and nearby coal mines. Whenever a recession or depression struck, factories shut down or laid off thousands of workers. Few could afford to save money from their meager wages. In order to survive, many turned to crime.

Despite his family's poverty, Allan was more fortunate than

most slum children because both his parents worked. His father was a weaver who became a corrections officer in the local jail. His mother worked in a spinning mill. Both of them insisted that their children get an education and make something of themselves. Allan's father was a strict man who disciplined his children. While Allan respected and perhaps feared his father, he was devoted to his mother and seems to have been her favorite child. When Allan was eight, his father died. Suddenly his school days were over and his working life began.

In the nineteenth-century children learned a trade by apprenticing themselves in an established business. Allan became an apprentice in a pattern-making shop owned by Neil Murphy, a good friend of his father's. But friendship did not make Allan's job any easier. He worked hard from sunrise to sunset, six days a week, for a few pennies a day. Although children were prohibited by law from working more than ten hours a day, the law was rarely enforced in the Gorbals. Throughout his life, Pinkerton would be haunted by the hardships of his childhood. Years later, he wrote: "Ah, the misery I think of since I have left Scotland . . . I can scarcely survive it, the misery and wretchedness of the Gorbals. It is terrible to think of what I escaped."

Even as a young child, Allan was determined to rise above the slums. After three years he quit his dreary job and apprenticed himself to William McCauley, a Glasgow cooper who taught him to make barrels. By the time Allan was eighteen, he was no longer an apprentice. He had proudly become a full-fledged member of the Coopers Association. He worked as a tramp cooper, traveling around the countryside making casks and barrels. He kept enough money to live on and sent the rest home to his mother.

Now a young man of medium height, Allan's job as a cooper

had made him extremely strong, with powerful arms and shoulders. He was not well educated and he was somewhat stubborn and dogmatic, but he had a sincere empathy for the sufferings of his fellow workers. Quiet, serious, somewhat withdrawn, but filled with enormous energy and drive, he was not afraid to speak out against injustice with passionate intensity if not eloquence. Yet at times it seemed that Pinkerton enjoyed physical conflict for its own sake rather than for what he considered a moral principle. There was a belligerent side to his personality—Pinkerton enjoyed a fight, and at times it seemed he didn't care if his opponent was friend or foe.

In 1838, Pinkerton became involved in a fierce struggle that developed between the working people of England and the rich and powerful land and factory owners who controlled the country. Hundreds of thousands of workers had joined a political movement called Chartism. At the heart of this movement was a document called the People's Charter, a petition demanding political reform. For centuries the aristocracy and merchants had successfully denied the right to vote to anyone who did not own sufficient property. Since most workers could not afford to own land or wealth, they were without direct representation in their government.

At first, the Chartists tried to peacefully persuade Parliament to pass the People's Charter into law. Among its provisions were the right of all men to elect their own representatives, the abolition of all property qualifications to vote, payment for members of Parliament so that poorer candidates could afford to run for office, and regularly scheduled elections. When the House of Commons rejected the bill, the Chartists split into two factions, the moral force men and the physical force men. As their names implied, the moral force faction sought to bring about passage of the Charter through peaceful means while the physical force supporters were ready to fight. Their motto was: "Peaceably if we can, forcibly if we must."

When the Chartist movement reached Scotland, Allan Pinkerton joined the physical force faction. The fight he hoped for was not long in coming. In the fall of 1839, the Welsh Chartists sent out a call for volunteers to help storm Monmouth Prison in Newport, Wales, and free Henry Vincent, one of their leaders, imprisoned there. Vincent had been seized for making radical speeches against the English government. Swinging his ten-pound cooper's hammer over his shoulder, Allan Pinkerton traveled several hundred miles from Glasgow to Wales. Although there is no record of how he got there, the most likely way would have been on foot. Allan had little money and people at that time traveled great distances by walking and hitching rides on horse-drawn wagons.

The leader of the raid was a former mayor and justice of the peace, John Frost. When Pinkerton arrived on the bitter-cold moors outside of Newport, he and his fellow Scots listened to Frost and other Chartists make fiery speeches against the English government. There was talk of revolution and promises that the raid on Newport would be the signal for a general uprising throughout England.

Under the plan of attack the men would join forces with two other groups and then march to Newport and attack the prison. That night, Pinkerton marched with five-thousand men from Wales, Scotland, Ireland, and England in the pouring rain to a field where they were to meet the others. Hour after hour they tramped through the cold and rain, covered only with thin blankets and ragged clothing. Younger men like Pinkerton were able to endure the hardships, but some of the older men, worn down by years of malnutrition and hard labor, became seriously ill.

Many of the Chartists were armed with obsolete weapons from long-ago wars. They carried ancient muskets, swords, and long poles called pikes, which were sharpened to a point at one end. Some carried picks, shovels, iron bars, clubs, or, like Pinkerton, hammers to serve as weapons or tools to break down the prison wall.

All through the night, Pinkerton stood in the field above the town of Newport, shivering with his fellow Chartists as they waited for the others to join them. But no one else arrived. Later, the other groups claimed they had lost their way, although many accused them of cowardice. Those who showed up were confident they could win without the others. They decided to sweep into Newport in a surprise attack, storm the prison, and free the prisoner.

As a mournful gray dawn spread across the sky, John Frost, waving his red shirt on a pick, gave the signal to charge. Shouting battle cries, thousands of men rushed down the steep hill and into the town. But they had been betrayed. British soldiers, hiding behind the closed shutters of a hotel, coolly watched the unsuspecting men charge into the town. As the Chartists raced past the hotel, the soldiers mercilessly raked their lines with rifle fire. The front line of the attackers was instantly cut down. Those behind them tried desperately to charge but were massacred where they stood. The survivors turned in panic and ran, leaving their dead, dying, and wounded behind them. Within minutes, all the Chartists were in full flight. Sadly, Allan Pinkerton made the long trip back to Scotland. Years later, when he spoke about that disaster he said, "It was a bad day, that morning. We returned to Glasgow by the back streets and the lanes more like thieves than honest workingmen."

The defeat of the Chartists at Newport did not defeat or discourage Allan. He continued to devote much of his time and energy to Chartism. He spoke out in meetings against the moral force faction and in favor of direct action. He supported Julian Harney, a radical Chartist and a friend of Karl Marx, who constantly preached revolution. Whenever there was a strike, Pinkerton and his fellow Chartists would help the strikers and their families by raising money for them. Staging a concert and selling tickets was one of the most popular fund-raising techniques of the times. Whenever a concert was held, it always sold out, especially if the funds went to help striking workers.

It was at one such concert that Allan Pinkerton heard a young woman named Joan Carfrae defiantly sing the Chartist anthem. The anthem had been banned by the English authorities and anyone singing it in public risked arrest. Pinkerton couldn't take his eyes off the young singer. He was moved not only by her beauty and wonderful voice but by her passionate dedication to Chartism. From then on, wherever she sang, Allan would turn up in the front row, wearing his best (and only) suit and his one good pair of shoes. He watched her with adoring eyes. "I got sort of hanging around her, clinging to her, so to speak, and I knew I couldn't live without her," he later said. But just as his romance was beginning to develop he learned that he had become "an outlaw, with a price on his head." A warrant had been issued for his arrest, and the police were looking for him. Allan had not committed any overt criminal act, but in those days, a person could be arrested for criticizing the government. Many Chartists had already been imprisoned for speaking out, and some had been exiled to Australia.

Warned of the warrant by friends, Allan decided to flee Scotland and sail for North America. But how could he leave behind the woman he loved? Fortunately Joan felt the same way about him. She begged some of Allan's friends to take her to where he was hiding. Allan Pinkerton never forgot that meeting:

> *When I had the price set on my head, she found me where I was hiding and when I told her I was all set up to make American barrels for the rest of my life and ventured it would be a pretty lonely business without my bonny singing bird around the shop, she just sang me a Scotch song that meant she'd go too, and God bless her, she did!*

Allan never explained why he chose to leave Scotland rather than stay and fight. Others were wanted by the police and yet they did not flee the country. Perhaps Allan did not want to risk having Joan arrested because of him. It was one of the few times in his life that he left a battlefield before the fight was finished.

Allan and Joan were married and smuggled out of the country on a boat bound for Nova Scotia, Canada. The ship, battered by the awesome storms of the North Atlantic, struck an iceberg off Nova Scotia and began to leak. While those aboard were saved, almost everyone, including Allan and Joan, lost their possessions.

In Canada, Allan looked for work as a barrel maker. For a few months he worked in Montreal, but when the job ended, he felt it was time to move to America. He bought tickets to Chicago on a steamer that crossed Lake Michigan between Canada and the United States. But Joan was deeply upset. She had put a small deposit on a hat and didn't want to leave Canada until she had gotten her money back. Allan raged but she insisted, and Allan angrily exchanged the tickets for a later date. For several days, he hardly spoke to her. Then one day she wordlessly spread a newspaper in front of him. The boiler on the steamer they had planned to ride had exploded as the ship was crossing the lake. Everyone on board was killed. From that day on, Allan promised "he'd let his wife have her way with hats."

2

A Little Job in the Detective Line

—————— 👁 ——————

When Joan and Allan Pinkerton first saw the little village of Dundee, Illinois, in 1843, they felt they had reached their promised land. They were drawn to the town by its beautiful country setting and because it had been founded by fellow Scots. Dundee had been named for its sister city in Scotland and the Scottish people living there maintained their old traditions. They performed the old songs and dances, taught the Gaellic language to their children, and kept alive the stories of their country's great battles.

Before settling in Dundee, Allan and Joan lived briefly in Chicago, but it was difficult for them to make a living there. For a short time Allan and his wife printed songbooks of old Scottish ballads. But by the spring of 1843, he was looking for a place to open his own business. Dundee was the perfect location.

The move to Dundee was a happy one for Allan and Joan. Their first child was born there and named William after Allan's father. Allan built a small house on a hill and opened up his own business as a barrel maker. Chicago was growing every day and trade was booming throughout the area. It seemed that the Pinkertons were destined to lead a prosperous, idyllic, and uneventful life.

But as peaceful and remote from the rest of the country as Dundee seemed, it was shaken by the great crisis over slavery that divided America in the 1840s. The abolitionist movement which had fiercely opposed slavery for the past fifteen years had supporters in Dundee. The cause strongly appealed to Allan and Joan. "I detested slavery. . . ," Pinkerton later wrote, ". . . believing it to be a curse to the American nation." He saw parallels between his Chartist days in Scotland and the struggle of blacks for liberation: "In my native country, I was free in name, but a slave in fact. I toiled night and day, and my labor went to sustain my government."

The Pinkertons joined the underground railroad—the network of abolitionists that helped slaves flee from bondage in the South to freedom in the North. By day, fugitives would be sheltered in the home of a member of the railway. By night, they would be guided farther north by abolitionists. They were always in danger for armed bounty hunters patrolled the roads to capture and return fleeing slaves for a reward.

From the time Allan and Joan Pinkerton joined the underground railroad, their lives were no longer their own. Fugitives would arrive at all hours of the night, seeking shelter, and needing to be fed and clothed. Allan taught many of them the craft of barrelmaking so they could eventually earn a living. The runaways told the Pinkertons harrowing tales of the cruelty they suffered under slavery and the terrors they experienced during their flight to freedom.

Even though Allan dedicated much of his time to the abolitionist movement, his business was prospering. His biggest problem was finding enough wood to use in his barrels. Fortunately he discovered a plentiful supply of trees on a deserted island in the nearby Fox River. This discovery changed the course of his life.

One day as he was gathering wood, Allan came across a deserted campfire and a charred piece of paper money. As he later wrote, "There was no picnicking in those days, people had more serious matters to attend to and it required no great keenness to conclude that no honest men were in the habit of occupying the place." Allan's curiousity was deeply aroused. The mystery began to obsess him. Who was using the island? And for what purposes? He began to visit the island regularly during the day, but saw no one, nor did he uncover fresh evidence that anyone had been there. Yet, he had a hunch something was wrong. He began to visit the island at night, hiding in the nearby bushes to see if anyone would show up. Night after night he waited fruitlessly. But he was a stubborn and determined man, and he felt that his efforts would pay off if he was patient. Then one night, as the moon was full, Allan saw a boat on the moonlit water glide towards the island. A group of laughing and drunken men piled out and building a campfire, began to talk. Allan tried to creep close enough to overhear them. While he could not make out their exact words, his sense of the conversation was that they were plotting a crime. The next day, Allan went to see the local Sheriff, Luther Dearborn, and told him what he had seen and heard. Dearborn was very concerned. He told Allan that a number of counterfeit gangs were operating in the area. Almost every merchant in town had been plagued by counterfeit bills, especially paper money. Counterfeiting was widespread at that time because each local bank printed its own money and most bills were relatively easy to copy. Dearborn asked Allan if he would help trap them. He enthusiastically agreed. Something within him had clicked, as if he had been called upon to do that for which he was destined.

Over a period of several weeks Allan, the Sheriff and several townspeople lay in wait for the suspects to return to the island. One dark night, just as Allan was beginning to fear that the men might have found another site, the boat appeared and landed on the island. Pinkerton and the others drew their guns and silently made their way to the campfire where the men had gathered. Surrounding them, they rushed out of the bushes and ordered everyone to put their hands up. Allan noticed that one of the men was trying to hide a small sack. He recovered it and when the bag was opened, he found it filled with counterfeit dimes.

The arrest of the counterfeiting gang brought Allan to the attention of two local merchants, I. C. Bosworth and H. E. Hunt. They approached Allan with an urgent request. "We have a little job in the detective line," they said. A stranger was in town asking where he might find the farm of a man reputed to be a counterfeiter. The merchants wanted Pinkerton to try to infiltrate the strangers gang, gather evidence of counterfeiting, and arrest the members. Allan laughed at their request. "Detective line?" he was quoted as saying "My line is the cooper business. What do I know about that sort of thing?'' But the merchants insisted that he was the right man for the job.

Allan protested that he also knew nothing about counterfeit money, and had never even seen a counterfeit bill. The merchants took him to their store, showed him two counterfeit ten-dollar bills from Smith's bank. and begged him to hurry to the harness shop where the stranger was having his saddle fixed.

Pinkerton pretended that he was a dumb country boy looking to make some quick and easy money. Barefoot and dressed in overalls, he went to the shop and admired the stranger's horse. The man asked Pinkerton if he knew the way to the house of Old Man Crane. Allan slyly nodded. He gave the stranger directions on how to get to Old Man Crane's house, and added that as

An illustration showing Pinkerton in disguise giving directions to Old Man Crane's.

far as he was concerned Old Man Crane was "as good as cheese,"—an expression that indicated that Allan knew of Crane's business and approved.

The stranger asked Allan to meet him later outside of town where they could talk in private. When they met, the man identified himself as John Craig, a Vermont farmer. He tested Pinkerton with many questions. Pinkerton told Craig that he was a barrelmaker and that times were hard. He deliberately gave Craig the impression that he was willing to do something illegal if it was safe and paid well.

Craig took the bait and asked Allan if he would be interested in making a few dollars by passing some "good bills" around. Craig offered to sell Allan five-hundred dollars in counterfeit money for one hundred-twenty-five dollars. Allan cautiously agreed but said he would have to go back to town to get the money.

After getting the money from the merchants, he then met Craig in the basement of an unfinished building and gave it to him. Craig told Pinkerton that he did not have the counterfeit bills with him, but if he would wait outside for a few minutes, his assistant would bring the money and place it under a rock. When Allan returned, he found the counterfeit money hidden where Craig said it would be. He believed that Craig himself had put it there.

Allan picked up the counterfeit money and was shocked to realize he wanted to keep it. "For a moment, the greatest temptation of my life swept over me. A thousand thoughts of sudden wealth and a life free from the grind of labor which I had always known came rushing to my mind," he later wrote. From that day on, he added. "I could never think of one undergoing the first great temptation to crime, whether he has resisted or fallen, without a touch of genuine human sympathy."

In order to trap Craig, Pinkerton arranged to meet him in a hotel in Chicago for another deal. Pinkerton's plan was to arrest Craig as soon as he turned over the money, but Craig had become suspicious of Pinkerton and didn't have any counterfeit money with him. Pinkerton arrested him anyhow, hoping that Craig could be convicted because he had given Pinkerton the five-hundred counterfeit dollars earlier. Although it seemed unlikely he would be convicted, Craig took no chances. Shortly after his arrest, Craig escaped from jail, "leaving behind a certain law officer who was much richer than he had been," Pinkerton later noted.

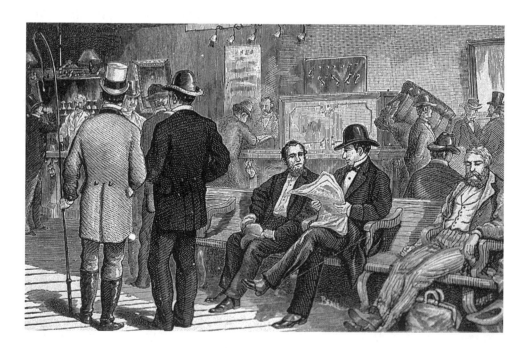

An illustration showing Pinkerton and Craig meeting in the hotel.

When Pinkerton returned to Dundee, Sheriff Dearborn offered him a job as deputy sheriff, which he accepted. In 1847, he decided to run for office on the abolitionist ticket. Although no record exists of the position he sought, it may have been for the state legislature. But his so-called "radical abolitionist views" led his local Baptist church to condemn him. They falsely accused him of being an atheist and a drinker. Angrily, the Pinkertons and their supporters left the church, but the damage was done and Pinkerton lost the election.

Pinkerton felt that his days in Dundee were over. Detective work had stirred a yearning for adventure within him and his thoughts turned to Chicago and the excitements of city life. When he was offered a job with the Chicago police force, he jumped at the chance.

3

The Eye That Never Sleeps

———— 👁 ————

As Allan Pinkerton returned home from work on a September evening in 1853, a gunman darted out of the shadows, fired two shots point blank into Pinkerton's back, and fled. Pinkerton fell to the ground, wounded. His habit of walking with his left hand tucked behind him under his coat saved his life. A Chicago newspaper described the attack: "The pistol was of a large caliber, heavily loaded and discharged so near that Mr. Pinkerton's coat was set on fire. Two slugs shattered the bone five inches from the wrist. . . ."

Pinkerton was not surprised that someone would try to kill him. From the time he first became a policeman in 1847 and then Chicago's first detective in 1850, he had made many enemies in the criminal underworld. He had earned a reputation as a fearless and uncorruptible police officer who relentlessly hunted down criminals, sometimes at great risk to his own life.

Pinkerton's diligence was unusual for a Chicago police officer in those days. The police force was outdated and organized on the archaic constable-watch system. During the day, twelve law officers known as constables tracked and returned stolen property, for which they received a reward. The ease with which they sometimes found stolen property led many to suspect they were in league with the robbers. At night, thirty-nine watchmen patrolled the streets. Their job was to make sure doors were locked, watch for robbers, and arrest drunks. Many watchmen were unreliable and some were actually more crooked than those they arrested.

Disgusted with the lack of professionalism by the police and the constant interference of politicians, Pinkerton resigned to take a job as Special United States Mail Agent for the post office. His first case was to investigate a case of mail theft plaguing the Chicago branch. Many businesses and private individuals were angrily complaining that money mailed to them was never received. It was obvious that someone inside the post office was stealing the mail.

Pinkerton went to work in the post office to see if he could spot a suspect. A clerk by the name of Theodore Dennison attracted his attention almost immediately because of the peculiar way he handled envelopes, different than the other clerks, it seemed to Pinkerton. He investigated the clerk and discovered that he had some expensive tastes for a man who earned a modest salary. He spent his evenings in the company of pretty women dining in Chicago's finest restaurants, drinking champagne, and dancing.

Pinkerton struck up a friendship with Dennison. He pretended to admire the way he worked and Dennison, flattered, boasted to Pinkerton that he could tell whether or not an envelope contained money—and how much—just by touching it with his fingers. Pinkerton also discovered that Dennison's brother also worked for a post office and had been caught stealing mail. However, both brothers were nephews of the postmaster, so Pinkerton had to proceed with caution.

After watching Dennison slip envelopes in his pockets from time to time, Pinkerton made his move. Although he did not know where Dennison hid the money he stole, he was sure that it was kept in his room at his boarding house. One day as Dennison was leaving the post office, Pinkerton made his move and arrested him. Dennison put up a fight, but Pinkerton subdued him and took him down to police headquarters. Then he informed the postmaster of the charges against his nephew. The postmaster was furious and told Pinkerton that he better have the evidence—or he would be fired.

Pinkerton and two deputies searched Dennison's room with the postmaster present. They examined the beds and chairs, ripping up the carpets and floor boards, but found nothing. Suddenly Pinkerton noticed the pictures on Dennison's wall. One of them was of the Virgin Mary. Pinkerton thought it highly unlikely that someone like Dennison would be sincere about religion. Pinkerton walked over to the picture and looked at it. He removed it from the wall and examined the front and back. Suddenly, he began to rip it apart, shocking everyone with what seemed to be a blasphemous act. But Pinkerton was right on target. Hidden behind the picture was fifteen hundred dollars in stolen money. He tore apart the other pictures and found more money. Dennison confessed and the case made headlines in the Chicago papers. One paper wrote: "As a detective Mr. Pinkerton has no superior and we doubt if he has any equal in the country."

Pinkerton's experience had taught him that it was difficult for an honest policeman to do his job without political interference. Yet, there was a great need for a good police force. Robbery, burglary, murder, and assault reached near epidemic proportions. People seldom went out at night. Stores, homes, churches, and railroads were constantly robbed. Among the many problems facing city and local police were corruption, incompetence, and their lack of authority to pursue a suspect outside of their area. Sometime around 1850—the exact date isn't clear—Pinkerton decided to open a private detective agency. However, he remained a police officer for at least two years before he was able to devote all his time to his new business.

By 1853, The Pinkerton Detective Agency was in full swing. It was the first national detective bureau in America which meant that its agents had the power to arrest criminals anywhere in the country. Pinkerton chose his detectives for their character rather than their experience as police officers. He selected men who were courageous, dedicated to the law, and incorruptible. His first employees included merchants and farmers; one was a watchmaker, another a chemist. He was impressed by their strong personalities and their keen powers of observation. There were many former Chicago policemen who sought positions with Pinkerton. But he rejected most of them because he feared their being on the force may have corrupted them.

One thing that Pinkerton did not have in mind was hiring a woman detective. But he soon changed his opinion after he met

Kate Warne. She had answered an ad Pinkerton had placed in the newspaper seeking detectives. At first, Pinkerton was amused. How could a woman be a detective, he wondered. "It was not the custom to employ women detectives," he told her. But the more he listened to Kate Warne, the more his amusement turned to respect. A woman could be most useful in "worming out secrets in many places in which it would be impossible for a male detective," Kate told him. Women could strike up a friendship with the wives and girlfriends of suspected criminals. Men tended to be boastful in a woman's presence. Also women were extremely keen observers. Pinkerton was convinced. The next day, he hired her. He never regretted his decision. "She succeeded far beyond my utmost expectations." Over the years, he would hire other women agents.

Pinkerton chose as the agency's motto, "The Eye That Never Sleeps," implying that the eyes of Pinkerton agents were always open, watching criminals and pursuing them until they were caught.

Pinkerton's motto and logo of an open eye.

Pinkerton set strict guidelines for his detectives and his agency. He would handle only those kinds of cases that the police were unable to solve—murders, robberies, counterfeiting, and confidence games. Neither his agents nor the agency could ever accept a reward for their services, other than their regular salaries and fees. The agency could never work for one political party against another, never spy on a government or labor official carrying out his duties, never investigate the morals of a woman, or infiltrate a closed union meeting. It was also an ironclad rule that the Pinkerton Agency would never take on divorce cases or cases involving quarrels between family members. However, several years after he opened his agency, Pinkerton—according to one of the detective novels based on his cases—once did make an exception and took on a very delicate case involving a husband and wife.

The case began when an attractive young woman, distraught and crying, appeared in the office of one of Pinkerton's superintendents, Frank Warner. She was well dressed and obviously wealthy, but she seemed as if she was on the verge of suicide. She reluctantly identified herself as Mrs. Saunders.

"It's my husband," she said, tearfully. "Some woman is breaking up our marriage." She went on to explain that she had been married for eighteen months and had a child. A few months ago she and her husband quarreled. "But instead of making up," she explained, "we both waited for the other to apologize." As a result, they stopped speaking to each other. Then they stopped having meals together. Finally, they began to sleep in separate parts of the house. Several weeks ago, Mrs. Saunders noticed that her husband was staying out all night long. She began to search for him late at night. "There must be another woman," she concluded. She begged Superintendent Warner to help her find out who this "horrible person" was, and convince her not to break up their home and ruin her life and that of her child.

The superintendent, although moved and sympathetic, said he could not help her. He explained that the Pinkerton detective agency had a policy of never taking cases involving husbands and wives. There were no exceptions. Mrs. Saunders begged and pleaded with the superintendent to ask Mr. Pinkerton if he would make an exception in her case. The woman was so distraught that he agreed.

That afternoon, Superintendent Warner went to see Allan Pinkerton in his office to discuss the case. Pinkerton was talking with a gentleman of obvious means who had come to discuss a personal matter. Pinkerton motioned for Warner to wait in the back of the room until they had finished talking. He explained to his visitor, whom he did not introduce, that the superintendent was one of his best men and very discrete.

The gentleman told Pinkerton his story. Eighteen months ago he had married a young woman from a very good family. They were madly in love and had a child a year after they were married. About three months ago they had a stupid quarrel and each waited for the other to apologize. When neither did, they stopped talking to each other. Several weeks ago he returned home from work very late and noticed that his wife was not in. Every night since then, he had been searching around the town trying to find out whom his wife had been seeing. The visitor begged Pinkerton to find the "fiend" who was destroying his home, and corrupting his wife and child. Pinkerton explained to the man that it was the company's policy not to take on quarrels between husbands and wives. However, he noticed a strange expression on his superintendent's face that indicated that he wanted to talk to Pinkerton alone. Pinkerton promised his visitor that he would give him an answer the following day.

When the man left, Superintendent Warner burst out laughing. He told Pinkerton the conversation he had with the man's wife that very morning. Pinkerton laughed and after a moment's thought, devised a plan to "solve" the case.

The next day, Superintendent Warner sent a note to Mrs. Saunders saying that after careful consideration, he had decided to take the case—and had, in fact, already solved it. He instructed her to come to his office as soon as possible. When she arrived, the Superintendent told her, "The guilty person will be here in fifteen minutes. I am going to put you in a private room where the two of you can talk things over." The woman protested, saying that she was afraid to meet this person face to face. She did not know what she could say to her. The superintendent replied that the only way to resolve the case was for her to meet her rival face to face, no matter how painful it might be. Reluctantly Mrs. Saunders agreed.

Meanwhile Allan Pinkerton had called on Mr. Saunders. He told him that he had found the person responsible for the trouble and, in fact, had the person in custody at his office. Pinkerton offered to take Mr. Saunders there on the condition that he promised not to get violent.

Superintendent Woods solemnly greeted Saunders and led him to the room where his wife waited. Pinkerton again cautioned Mr. Saunders against violence, the two detectives stepped back, and Saunders braced himself, opened the door, and discovered his wife. She was equally astonished. She turned to Superintendent Woods for an explanation. But he and Pinkerton had discreetly disappeared, closing the door behind them. Suddenly, they understood . . . they fell into each others arms, embraced and reconciled.

Although Pinkerton's employees considered him a humorless man, he could not resist the opportunity to play a good practical joke on his agents. He was once called in to solve a series of grave robberies in a small cemetery in Chicago. He stationed seven of his men and himself in the graveyard at night and waited for the robbers to return. When no one showed up after a week, Pinkerton wondered if the robbers had been tipped off to his presence. He decided to check on his men to see if anyone might be unintentionally revealing himself.

One of Pinkerton's guards was extremely superstitious and the longer he sat in the graveyard, the more nervous he became. When he thought no one was looking, he would try to overcome his fears by smoking his pipe and sipping whiskey. When Pinkerton discovered this, he was furious. He realized that the reason the robbers didn't show up was because the guard was alerting them by the glow and smoke of his pipe. Pinkerton was determined to teach him a lesson and, knowing of his fear of graveyards, also have some fun.

One dark night, when the wind was whistling through the cemetery, and the guard more frightened than ever, a low moan came from behind one of the tombstones. The guard became terrified. Sweat poured down his face. His knees knocked together. His eyes began to role in his head. "Who's there?" he called out in terror. Suddenly, from behind a tombstone, a white, ghostly form appeared and slowly advanced towards the trembling guard. With a yell and a cry, he jumped to his feet and ran through the cemetery leaping over tombstones, mounds of dirt, open graves, and bushes. The "ghost" followed close behind him. The other agents began to run after him, firing their pistols in the air—thinking that the thieves had been caught. The guard leaped over the wall surrounding the graveyard, ran down the street, and disappeared. The "ghost" pursued the fleeing man through the empty streets of Chicago before he finally stopped and took off his sheet. It was Allan Pinkerton. His intention was to teach the guard a lesson about smoking and drinking on duty. But the lesson was learned too well. That night, the guard left town without even stopping to get his belongings or pay. He was never again seen in Chicago.

Pinkerton plays his prank.

4

Can You Send a Man, Half-Horse, Half-Alligator?

W hen Allan Pinkerton first visited Chicago in 1842, it was little more than a country village of about 1,200 people. Nine years later, when he started his detective agency there, Chicago had been transformed by the railroad into a major city of 35,000 people. Miles of track linked Chicago with the Midwest, South and Northeast. Trains carried wheat, vegetables, cotton, cattle, and hogs to Chicago from the Great Plains and Gulf states, and transported meat and grains to Boston and New York. Railroads not only transported products, they transported people and money. They carried tens of thousands of settlers to the West and shipped millions of dollars in gold and currency across the country.

The railroads also gave rise to a new breed of criminal—the outlaws. In the beginning, they terrorized passengers and robbed railway safes with impunity. Local sheriffs and law enforcement officials lacked the means to prevent hold-ups and the authority to chase outlaws beyond their jurisdiction. There was no national police force to pursue them across state borders.

Almost immediately after opening his office, Pinkerton was employed by the railroads. His first assignments were investigating petty crimes such as passengers sneaking free rides or conductors pocketing ticket money. But he was destined for larger things.

In 1854 he received a letter from the Adams Express Company, the nation's largest shipper of gold and money by rail. Written by Edward S. Sanford, the company's vice-president, the letter described the loss of $10,000 from a locked money pouch that had disappeared somewhere between Montgomery, Alabama, and Augusta, Georgia. Based on information contained in Sanford's letter, Pinkerton concluded that the thief must be the manager of the company's Montgomery office, Nathan Maroney. He advised Sanford to keep Maroney under surveillance "before he bites you twice."

Sanford did not immediately reply. Then some months later a telegram arrived. It read: "Can you send a man, half-horse, half-alligator? I got bit once more."

The Nathan Maroney case was a turning point in Pinkerton's career. It made him famous and gave him the chance to develop investigative techniques he would later use to solve a number of crimes.

Pinkerton arrived in Montgomery where he learned from Sanford that this time $40,000 had been stolen from the company. Again, Nathan Maroney was the prime suspect. Although there was no real evidence against him, the company had charged him with the crime and Maroney had been arrested by local authorities. However, both Maroney and his wife were very popular and their friends vigorously protested his arrest. To the surprise of the express company, a sympathetic judge let Maroney go free on relatively low bail. Sanford told Pinkerton he feared the company may have made a serious mistake in arresting Maroney.

Pinkerton immediately summoned his best agents, including Kate Warne, Frank Roche (whose favorite disguise was that of a German-speaking farmer), John Fox, a former watchmaker turned detective, and John White, a detective who could expertly play the role of a thief.

Pinkerton first sent Roche to follow Mrs. Maroney. He dressed like a country farmer in baggy pants and an old cap, and smoked a large, curved pipe. When Mrs. Maroney took a trip through the South, Roche was able to follow her without arousing her suspicions. He even managed to intercept several letters she mailed and discovered that she planned to visit relatives in Jenkinstown, Pennsylvania.

Immediately Pinkerton sent Kate Warne and John Fox to Jenkinstown before Mrs. Maroney arrived. Fox set up a watch shop as a base of operations, while Kate took a room at a local boardinghouse and pretended to be the wife of a wealthy forger. Her assignment was to make friends with Mrs. Maroney when she arrived and win her confidence.

Meanwhile, a break in the case developed when one of Pinkerton's superintendents, George Bangs, learned that Maroney had been in contact with a locksmith in New York. Pinkerton visited the locksmith, who admitted he had made copies of a key for Maroney, and still had one in his possession. Even though the key belonged to Adams Express Company, the company's lawyer still felt they lacked sufficient evidence to bring the case to trial. Pinkerton then suggested arresting Maroney on a conspiracy charge outside of Alabama so that he would not have friends to help him or sufficient funds for bail. Although reluctant, the express company agreed and when Maroney visited New York, Pinkerton had him arrested and jailed. He then arranged for detective John White to also be "arrested" as a forger and placed in the same cell with Maroney.

Now the stage was set for Pinkerton's little drama to unfold. Kate Warne began to successfully cultivate the friendship of Mrs. Maroney. At the same time, Pinkerton had another of his agents pretend to woo Mrs. Maroney while he sent anonymous notes to her husband in jail about his wife's flirtation. Maroney was deeply upset. He was afraid that his wife might run off with this stranger and take the money with her, although White was not sure which concerned Maroney more—his wife or the money. Maroney confided to White that he needed to get out of jail. White told Maroney that he might be able to arrange it but it would cost money. To prove his point, White arranged for his own release through his "lawyer," who was another Pinkerton agent. Convinced that White could arrange his release. Maroney sent word to his wife to turn over the money to him.

When Mrs. Maroney received her husband's request, she was uncertain what to do. The only person she felt she could trust was Kate Warne. Kate told her that it was in her own best interests to give the money to White. When he arrived in Jenkinstown, Mrs. Maroney handed him the Adam's Express sack containing the $40,000 minus $400 Mrs. Maroney had taken for expenses. White immediately took the money to Pinkerton. Pinkerton then instructed White to continue his friendship with Maroney until his trial. When the trial began, the first witness the prosecutor called to testify against Maroney was John White. Maroney nearly fainted in court when he saw his former cellmate walk up to the witness stand. He immediately changed his plea to guilty and was sentenced to ten years in prison. His wife received a suspended sentence, and Pinkerton was put on retainer by the express company.

While Pinkerton's methods would be considered simplistic today, they were innovative for their time. He was able to use these techniques successfully because criminals were unfamiliar with them. But fame did not come solely from his use of disguises. Fame came from his reputation as the detective who got his man. He pursued criminals with fierce determination. It was the rare criminal that got away when Pinkerton fixed his eye on him. Pinkerton and his agents would follow a suspect to the end of the earth. They chased criminals on foot, horseback, mule, train, carriage, or boat. Using as many detectives as he needed, Pinkerton would not rest until he had both caught the thief and recovered the stolen goods.

Perhaps Pinkerton's greatest contribution to law enforcement in America was that he helped make police detection a science. Before the FBI was founded in 1908 there was no national bureau from which local law-enforcement officials could get information about criminals. Pinkerton organized a rogue's gallery that contained photographs and detailed information about known criminals and outlaws. He would list their physical characteristics, such as scars, moles, hair, eye color, height, weight, and any noticeable defects or birthmarks. He would list each criminal's speciality, e.g., bank robber, confidence man, train robber, how and with whom they liked to work, their favorite places and methods of operation, their likes and dislikes, and the names of their friends, family, and associates.

Pinkerton believed in phrenology, a nineteenth-century pseudoscience that claimed the personality of an individual was revealed by the shape and bumps on the human head. Phrenologists believed that biology determined criminal behavior and claimed that they could determine criminal types by analyzing the head and features of a person. But while Pinkerton may have believed in phrenology, there is no evidence that he arrested anyone on the basis of his beliefs.

Pinkerton was constantly sharing information from his files with law enforcement officials throughout the country. They, in turn, usually gave the Pinkertons' full cooperation since Pinkerton would not allow his agency or his detectives to receive rewards, when the agents caught their man, they usually turned him over to local authorities, who then collected the reward themselves.

As Pinkerton's business grew in the 1850s, so did his family. He now had five children, William the eldest, twins Robert and Joan, Belle, Mary, and Elizabeth. Mary and Elizabeth died young and Belle was an invalid most of her life. Pinkerton's mother and brother Robert had come over from Scotland to live with him. In 1854, his mother died.

Pinkerton considered himself a strict parent. Within his family and his business Allan's word was law. He ran his life in a military fashion. He was up before dawn, took cold baths and long walks, and went to bed early. He would not allow cards and alcohol in his house, although later on he stocked an excellent wine cellar for his guests. When his children grew up, they considered him a tyrant and fought against his oppressive ways. Yet, despite the conflicts, the family ties were never severed.

While Pinkerton was very moral, he was not religious. He considered himself an "infidel." He was also aware of some of his limitations. "I had not an education," he wrote, "and can scarcely read, but I have made human nature my study."

Work and the underground Railroad were the center of Pinkerton's life. He was away from home for long periods of time and the major responsibility of bringing up the children fell on Joan. She not only cared for the house, the children, and her in-laws, but often fed and sheltered fugitive slaves who appeared at their home when Allan was away. While not too much is known about her, she seems to have accepted Allan's domination and later, when the quarrels developed between her husband and her children, she would take to bed rather than take sides.

Pinkerton could be stubborn, opinionated, selfish, and egotistical. He once wrote: "I feel no power on earth is able to check me, no power in Heaven and Hell can influence me when I know I am right." Yet he could be generous when the occasion called for it. If a criminal wanted to start an honest life, Pinkerton would extend a helping hand. And despite the fact that he dominated his family, he was especially grieved by the deaths of two of his children. He expressed his anguish in a letter to his wife, in which he acknowledged his great debt to her:

"I felt it much," he wrote, "but I know how deeply you felt it. We remember the days of their birth as well as the last day we had them on earth . . . I know, since you were eighteen years of age, you have

been battling with me side by side, willing to do anything, bear our children, and work hard, yet you never found fault, you never said a cross word but was always willing to make our home cheery and happy . . ."

By the late 1850s Allan Pinkerton had achieved considerable fame and success and was friendly with some of the most influential people in Chicago including a lawyer named Abraham Lincoln. It would seem that he would have put behind him the days of his radical youth. But his personal prosperity did not make him change his feelings about slavery. He hated it more than ever.

5

I Had Always Been a Man After the John Brown Stamp

— 👁 —

The crisis over slavery brought the country to the brink of civil war. The South demanded a guarantee that slavery would continue to be allowed in the states where it was already established and permitted to spread to new territories in the Midwest and West. They also wanted the North to return any slaves who fled there. Many Northerners wanted to stop the spread of slavery altogether, not necessarily because they were sympathetic to the suffering of slaves, but because they did not want blacks in their states.

Moderate Southerners and Northerners, in Congress, tried to heal the growing bitterness by working out a series of compromises. They passed a bill known as the Compromise of 1850. It permitted slavery to expand to some new territories. One provision of the bill was the Fugitive Slave Act, which made it a federal crime for slaves to run away and a crime for anyone to assist them. This meant that Allan Pinkerton could be arrested and imprisoned for his underground activities. Pinkerton did not waver. He continued to help fugitives find safety in Canada, joining forces with John Brown, the most radical abolitionist of his time, a man willing to go to any extreme to end slavery.

John Brown

In 1855, when John Brown arrived in Kansas, it was a territory on the verge of civil war. A bitter quarrel had broken out over whether Kansas should be admitted to the Union as a free state or a slave state. Bands of raiders on both sides patrolled the roads day and night, killing and robbing one another. The anti-slavery riders were called Jayhawkers—named after birds that robbed other birds. The proslavery gunmen were known as Border Ruffians, and most came from the neighboring slave state of Missouri.

John Brown and his sons plunged right into the conflict. When five anti-slavery men were slaughtered by border ruffians, John Brown felt called upon by God to take revenge. On the night of May 24, 1856, Brown, with four of his sons and three of his followers, suddenly appeared outside the home of James Doyle on Pottawatomie Creek in south Kansas. Doyle was reputed to be a pro-slavery man. Brown and his men burst into the house armed with rifles and swords. Doyle's wife, terrified that something horrible was about to happen, offered Brown and the others food and drink in hopes of appeasing them. Brown politely refused. He said that he had come on other business and dragged Doyle and his two oldest sons outside. Brown's men shot Doyle dead, and split open the skulls of his sons with their broadswords. They returned to the house to kill the youngest boy, who was sixteen, but his mother pleaded with Brown to spare his life. He granted her wish, but his night of vengeance was not over. By daybreak Brown and the others had killed two other pro-slavery men.

Although they were now wanted men with prices on their heads, Brown and his followers continued to operate in Kansas throughout 1856. They raided the homes of slave owners, freeing their slaves and taking their cattle and horses. Before leaving Kansas, they freed eleven slaves, whom they took with them. Brown and his band then headed north to freedom across the plains of Kansas during a bitter cold winter. The thousand mile journey was incredibly grueling. They evaded a posse seeking to lynch them, crossed icy rivers and overflowing streams, suffered frostbite, and illness. Finally, Brown and his exhausted party arrived at the door of the one man with whom they knew they would be safe—Allan Pinkerton! Without hesitation he took them in: He remembered that day all his life:

"I was awakened about half past four in the morning. I partly dressed myself and went to the door. On opening it, who stood in the door but John Brown himself. I can recollect him very well, even now . . . well built, tall, straight as an arrow, his hair rather white. Beyond him I could see a crowd of white and colored men, women and children standing on the street. The men had rifles."

Why did Pinkerton help John Brown? Why did he not consider him a criminal, especially since Brown was a murderer? Some people believed that Pinkerton was unaware of the killings. But many years later, when the story of Brown's slaughter was well known, Pinkerton still proclaimed his friendship with John Brown. "I had always been a man after the John Brown stamp," he said, "aiding slaves to escape, or keeping them employed or running them into Canada when in danger."

Pinkerton's past as a member of the Chartist movement makes it clear that it was not unusual for him to support what he thought were just causes. He had strong ideas about right and wrong. He considered a man who robbed or murdered for profit a common criminal. However, someone who did the same thing for a noble cause could be a hero. One man said of him, "While Pinkerton's right hand caught lawbreakers, his left hand broke the law." But for Allan Pinkerton there was no conflict. Slavery was wrong in the eyes of God and man, and anything he could do to free slaves he would do, legal or not.

When Brown and his followers arrived at the Pinkertons' home, Allan and Joan immediately fed and clothed everyone and found safe places for them to stay. Pinkerton then called upon a fellow abolitionist, Colonel C. G. Hammond, superintendent of the Illinois Central Railroad, to arrange a railroad car to smuggle the fugitives to safety in Canada. Hammond agreed, but Brown needed five hundred dollars for their expenses before they could leave. Pinkerton was willing to put up part of the money, but he could not afford the whole amount. He was aware that a Democratic convention was then in session to select a candidate for the Cook County circuit judge. He knew many of the people gathered there and was well known by most of them, not only for his detective work but for his strong abolitionist views. Many of the delegates Pinkerton knew were sympathetic to the abolitionist cause.

Pinkerton went to the convention, stood up on the stage, and in a loud voice explained that John Brown was in town with eleven fugitives and needed five hundred dollars to get them to Canada. A local paper reported his speech: "Gentlemen, I have one thing to do and I intend to do it in a hurry. John Brown is in this city with a number of men, women, and children. I require substantial aid. . . . I am ready and willing to leave this meeting if I get this money; if not, I will bring John Brown to this convention and if any United States marshal lays hands on him, he must take the consequences. I am determined to do this, for I must have the money." After Pinkerton's speech, there was a long silence. Then a well-known politician, John Wilson, rose and handed Pinkerton fifty dollars. Soon other delegates came up and placed money in Pinkerton's hat. In a short time Pinkerton had his money and left the convention. Taking his pistol, he and his son William gathered everyone in a wagon and took them to the railroad terminal. As their train departed Allan turned to his son and said, "Look well upon that man, Willy. He is greater than Napoleon and as great as George Washington."

Pinkerton and Brown never met again. Later that year John Brown and his men attacked the federal arsenal at Harpers Ferry, Virginia, in hopes of starting a slave uprising in the South. The raid failed and most of the attackers were killed or captured. Brown was captured and, although severely wounded, he was tried and convicted for insurrection and sentenced to death by hanging. Pinkerton desperately tried to free Brown. He persuaded influential people to pressure President James Buchanan to commute Brown's sentence. In later writings Pinkerton hinted that he had even considered organizing an attack on the jail where Brown was imprisoned. But Brown died a martyr's death on the gallows and passed into American legend. Many believe that his acts and his death were the sparks that set the fires of civil war. When the war began, Allan Pinkerton would finally put his detective skills into the service of his abolitionist beliefs.

6

Plums Arrives Safely With Nuts

---- 👁 ----

It was a gray, gloomy February day in Springfield, Illinois, in the year 1861. A cold rain had been falling all morning. A tall, thin man, whose face seemed as melancholy as the day, boarded a train that would take him two-thousand miles away to Washington, D.C. Abraham Lincoln was on his way to be inaugurated as the sixteenth President of the United States. En route, he would stop at almost a dozen cities to address hundreds of thousands of people. Waiting for him near the end of his journey in the city of Baltimore, Maryland, were a band of Southern radicals planning to kill him. The only man that stood in their way was Allan Pinkerton.

Lincoln's election had triggered an outburst of rage throughout the South. Some radicals had threatened civil war while others demanded that the Union be dissolved and the Southern states form their own government. The Southern press viciously attacked Lincoln, calling him a baboon, a tyrant, and a dictator. Some journalists claimed that it would be better to have the devil as President rather than Lincoln.

Southerners hated Lincoln because they feared he would abolish slavery. Yet even though Lincoln was personally opposed to slavery, he was unwilling to do much to change it. While he stated in one of his speeches that this nation could not exist "half slave and half free," Lincoln also said that he had no intention of ending slavery in those states where it already existed. Lincoln's hope was that slavery would die a natural death over a period of time.

But the South was not willing to let slavery die at all. For almost two-hundred years the Southern states had been joined to slavery in unholy matrimony. Slavery was the life blood of the Southern economy. Slaves planted and tilled the crops, took care of the houses, built and repaired tools and equipment, and raised the children of their owners. Most slave owners were willing to secede from the United States rather than run the risk of having their slaves freed.

While many Southerners hoped that the South could separate peacefully from the North, a few Southern radicals were eager for a civil war. These "fire eaters," as they were called, felt that the only way to protect themselves from the North was to destroy its armies on the battlefield. They were willing to go to any extreme to begin the battle, including assassinating the President of the United States.

While technically a Northern state, Maryland was deeply

divided in it sympathies. The southern part of the state was controlled by slave owners, many of whom were Southern radicals willing to take desperate action. The northern part was inhabited by those people opposed to slavery. The side that controlled Baltimore also controlled the fate of Washington, D.C., as the President would have to pass through the city on his way to Washington, a fact that Lincoln's would-be assassins knew well.

By coincidence Allan Pinkerton was already in Baltimore with three of his top agents, Harry Davies, Timothy Webster, and Hattie Lawton. Pinkerton was on a secret mission for the Wilmington and Baltimore Railroad, which had received many threats to destroy its tracks, tunnels, bridges, and trains in and around Baltimore. The railroad provided a direct line between the North and Washington, D.C., and was of vital military importance in case of war. Pinkerton's job was to find out if there were plans to sabotage the railroad and if so, break up the conspiracy.

Pinkerton and Hattie Lawton opened up a stockbroker office in a building in Baltimore. Pinkerton then sent Harry Davies to live in a hotel where many radical Southerners congregated. Timothy Webster and Hattie Lawton were sent to Perryville, a town outside of Baltimore where Pinkerton had learned that a group of Southerners who were still officers in the United States Army were plotting against the government.

Each agent pretended to be a strong Southern sympathizer and within a short time they found themselves within the inner circles of conspirators. Pinkerton made contact with a fellow stockbroker by the name of Luckett (his first name was not recorded in Pinkerton's account of the case). Luckett quickly hinted to Pinkerton that the Southerners in Baltimore would soon strike a blow for the South. At first Pinkerton thought Luckett was talking about blowing up the railroad. But Luckett was not interested in the railroad. What he was interested in was its passenger—Abraham Lincoln! Luckett believed that Lincoln was a tyrant and that soon he would "suffer the fate of all tyrants." Pinkerton pretended to be sympathetic to his causes and gave Luckett some money. Luckett promised Pinkerton that he would introduce him to some men who were ready "to act boldly."

Meanwhile Harry Davies struck up a friendship with a young Southern aristocrat, O. K. Hillard. Hillard came from a prominent family in South Carolina and Davies reported to Pinkerton that Hillard was an honorable man, brave, and chivalrous. He was also a heavy drinker, a playboy, charming, and blindly devoted to the South. Davies put Hillard's fondness for liquor to good use. He continually took him drinking and the more Hillard drank, the more he talked. Davies was seeking to learn about plots against the railroad and, like Pinkerton, was astonished to discover hints of a plot against Lincoln. Hillard openly expressed a deep hatred of Lincoln and said that "he was willing to die to rid his country of a tyrant such as Lincoln." He predicted to Davies that Lincoln would die in Baltimore. When Davies asked how Lincoln could be killed when there would be police protection around him Hillard confided to Davies that the chief of police, Colonel George Kane, was a strong Southern man. He had already refused to provide an escort for Lincoln should he want to parade through Baltimore on his way to Washington. When Davies pressed Hillard to find out if there was a plot, Hillard suddenly became silent. However, he promised Davies he would introduce him to a man named Cypriano Ferrardini when the time was ripe.

Actually, Pinkerton had already met Ferrardini through

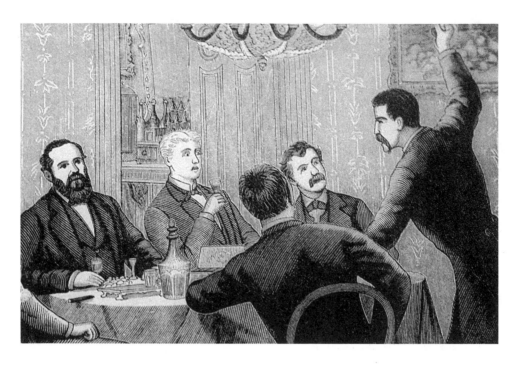

Pinkerton, with a beard on the left, learns of the plot to assassinate President Lincoln.

Luckett at a restaurant. At first, Ferrardini was suspicious of Pinkerton. To win his confidence, Pinkerton threw suspicion on two men having dinner nearby, although he hadn't the faintest idea who the men were. Pinkerton's caution impressed the others. As Pinkerton and the conspirators had dinner, he ordered a lot of wine. Pinkerton, who refused to allow a drop of liquor in his home and strongly disapproved of drinking, could become a very social drinker when on a case. He was aware that many men were insulted if a man in their company did not drink with them.

Finally, as dinner neared its ends, the wine and Pinkerton's charm began to take effect. Ferrardini finally revealed his intention of assassinating Lincoln. He boasted that arrangements had been made to kill the President after his train arrived at Baltimore on the afternoon of February 22. The plot was simple: Lincoln would have to change trains once he arrived in Baltimore. Since the train to Washington was located at a different station he would need a police guard to escort him from one station to the other. However, many of the officers guarding him were Southern sympathizers and would not protect him from an attack. The conspirators would strike when Lincoln arrived at the second station. Pinkerton later quoted Ferrardini as saying, "Some of our men will begin a fake fight—to draw off the police. Lincoln will be unguarded. Then the rest of our men will strike the tyrant down with their daggers and revolvers. In the confusion that follows, they will escape in a boat which will take them to Virginia." Ferrardini concluded by vowing, "Lincoln shall die in this city."

The plan shocked Pinkerton. His next move was to find out who would actually do the killing. Davies was able to accompany O. K. Hillard to a secret meeting of the conspirators. There, in a darkened room, some thirty men gathered to see who would be chosen to carry out Lincoln's murder. It was agreed that the men would draw ballots from a box. All the ballots would be white, except one, which would be red. Whoever drew the red ballot would kill the President. However, those who planned the draw put in eight red ballots instead of one. They reasoned that if only one person drew a red ballot, he might weaken at the last moment. By putting eight red ballots in the box, the odds were greater that someone would carry out the assassination. Since everyone was pledged to secrecy, no one would know there was more than one red ballot.

As Pinkerton and Davies uncovered this plot against Lincoln,

This illustration shows the moment when the conspirators against Lincoln are pledged to secrecy before drawing their ballots.

Timothy Webster discovered another. In Perryville, he met and became friends with a group of Southern officers in the United States Army. Webster learned that they were planning to blow up the train that was carrying Lincoln before it reached Baltimore. Once Lincoln was killed, they would cut the telegraph wires and destroy bridges and tracks to prevent Northern troops from arriving in the city!

Pinkerton met with his agents to compare notes. Though he had no doubt that the President was in danger, he felt there was not enough evidence to convict the conspirators in court. Moreover, since the chief of police was a strong Southern supporter, Pinkerton felt that revealing the plot to the police would accomplish nothing. The plotters would probably be treated as heroes and Pinkerton and his agents might themselves be assassinated. Instead, Pinkerton concluded that Lincoln must be warned immediately and steps taken to protect him.

Lincoln had arrived in Philadelphia and was due in Baltimore in two days. Pinkerton immediately traveled to Philadelphia to warn the President, but there were so many people surrounding him, that Pinkerton could not get to see him. Finally Pinkerton convinced one of Lincoln's closest advisers of the danger. Late that night, Pinkerton finally met with Lincoln and several of his advisers and laid out what he had uncovered. Lincoln calmly dismissed Pinkerton's report. He pointed out that there were rumors all the time about people wanting to kill him. If he changed his plans every time he heard a rumor, he would never get to Washington.

However, the President's advisers felt that he should listen to Pinkerton. There had been many reports of plots against the President in Baltimore. It was not worth taking a chance. If Lincoln were to be killed, war would be inevitable.

Lincoln turned to Pinkerton for advice. Pinkerton suggested that Lincoln go to Washington as planned—but at a different time than originally scheduled. Pinkerton urged Lincoln to leave immediately for Washington and arrive at night rather than during the day. Lincoln reluctantly agreed to the late arrival, but refused to leave right away. He had to go to Harrisburg, Pennsylvania, to give an important speech and, despite Pinkerton's pleas, would not change his plans.

Pinkerton spent the next twenty-four hours making all the arrangements for the President's trip. He arranged a news blackout about the President's travel plans. In order not to attract attention, he arranged for the President to travel on the regular midnight train to Baltimore rather than a special one. As soon as Lincoln left Harrisburg to return to Philadelphia, Pinkerton had the telegraph wires cut so that no one could send a message reporting that the President had departed. He arrived in Philadelphia at 10 P.M. Pinkerton had a carriage drive him around the city until the train was ready to leave. Shortly after eleven o'clock, Lincoln, wearing a dark hat and coat, boarded the train. One of Lincoln's advisers offered him a revolver and bowie knife. Pinkerton was furious. "If there is any fighting, *we* will do it," he said. Lincoln turned the weapons down and said that it was bad enough to have to sneak into the Capitol like a thief in the night, but to do so armed would make him look like a fool and a coward.

At midnight, the train departed for Baltimore. All along the route, Pinkerton placed his agents with lanterns. As the train approached, the agents swung their lanterns to signal that the track ahead was clear. Throughout the trip, Pinkerton remained tense while the President was in a good mood, telling jokes and funny stories.

The trip to Baltimore went smoothly. Once inside the city Pinkerton and his men prepared for the worst. The President was quickly led to a waiting carriage, which immediately set off down the empty Baltimore streets. Occasionally, they passed drunken men singing anti-Union songs, completely unaware that the President was passing by. Throughout the trip Pinkerton's hand was on his gun. Twenty minutes later the carriage arrived at the station where the train for Washington was waiting. But there was no one to unlock the gate and let them on board. Immediately Pinkerton suspected a trap, but the problem was resolved when they finally located a night watchman. He told them that the conductor who had the keys was asleep in a nearby building. The night watchman banged on the door with his club to wake him up. The conductor slept through the noise. Pinkerton watched the streets, his gun ready as Lincoln, relaxed, laughed with the watchman. After twenty minutes of pounding, the conductor finally woke up and let the President and Pinkerton board the train.

At six o'clock the next morning, the train arrived safely in Washington. But as Lincoln walked through the railroad station a man reached out and grabbed the President by the arm. Pinkerton immediately struck the man who protested that he was a friend of the President. Just as Pinkerton was ready to hit him again, Lincoln stopped him and told Pinkerton that the man was an old friend of his named Washburne.

"Plums arrives safely with Nuts." The bearded man with the shawl is this illustrator's rendition of President Lincoln, accompanied by Allan Pinkerton.

Immediately after their safe arrival, Pinkerton sent a coded telegram to Philadelphia letting everyone know that the President arrived safely. Unfortunately, he had not given much thought to the code names he had chosen for himself and the President. He had called himself Plums and the President Nuts. And so his message to Philadelphia read "Plums arrives safely with Nuts."

Although Lincoln was safe in Washington, his critics and opponents accused him of cowardice for traveling in secrecy. There were some who later claimed that there was never any real threat to the President's life and that Pinkerton made it up to further his own career. Yet the evidence shows that the danger of assassination was very real. Shortly after the President's arrival, Southern rebels in Baltimore attacked the railroad and caused considerable damage. The country seemed to be caught in a giant whirlpool and was going down.

7

I Heard the Sound of a Kiss

———— 👁 ————

As Allan Pinkerton rushed Abraham Lincoln through the Washington railway terminal in the hours before dawn on February 23, the storm clouds of war were gathering over the nation. Seven Southern states, South Carolina, Mississippi, Florida, Alabama, Georgia, Louisiana and Texas, had already seceded from the Union and formed the Confederate States of America. Soon Virginia and Tennessee would join them.

Lincoln was conciliatory toward the South while remaining firm in his refusal to accept their secession. In his inaugural address of March 4, 1861, he insisted that the Southern states return to the Union. Lincoln again repeated his committment not to interfere with slavery where it already existed and to enforce the unpopular fugitive slave law in the North. He even promised he would not invade Southern territory. But Lincoln's plea fell on deaf ears.

The capital was filled with intrigue as the country moved closer to war. Washington was basically a Southern city and slaves were bought and sold under the shadow of the White House. Southern men dominated the political life of the city and Southern women dominated its social life. Their parties and balls were attended by both Northern and Southern senators and congressmen, generals and young officers, administrators and cabinet members. Some Southern women were personally involved with men who had access to important military and political secrets.

Allan Pinkerton was keenly aware that the city was filled with spies. He was opposed to any compromise with the South and welcomed war as a necessary evil to end slavery. He met with the President and offered to create a secret service to uncover and arrest Southern spies and plotters. The President was interested but noncommittal. He still hoped that the South might rejoin the Union and he did not want to provoke further hostility by arresting prominent Southerners.

Discouraged and angered by Lincoln's seeming indifference, Pinkerton started to return to Chicago when he received a telegram from his close friend George McClellan. McClellan had been Vice President of the Illinois Central railroad and had hired Pinkerton to investigate railway thefts and robberies. Before joining the railroad, however, McClellan had been an officer in the Union army. He had served with distinction in the Mexican war and had earned the reputation as an outstanding leader, a man who could transform raw recruits into excellent soldiers.

Although he was a short, vain, pompous man, he was loved by
the soldiers he commanded and was affectionately called "Little
Mac" by them. As war approached, Lincoln appointed McClellan
general of the army of Ohio.

McClellan wanted Pinkerton to set up a military intelligence
operation and dispatch his agents into the South. Pinkerton
himself traveled through parts of the South under the name of
E.J. Allen. He pretended to be a Southerner in favor of rebellion.
His pretense was successful at first, but he was recognized in

**Pinkerton, in the checked shirt, and his detectives set up base camp to
begin their intelligence operation.**

Memphis, Tennessee. A black porter risked his life to save Pinkerton from capture by sneaking into his hotel room and warning him that soldiers were on their way to arrest him. The porter helped Pinkerton escape down the back stairs before the soldiers arrived.

In Alabama, Pinkerton had an even closer shave when he went to a barbershop for a haircut. It turned out that the barber recognized Pinkerton as a customer in Chicago.

"Mr. Binkerton, how gut to see you," the barber called out in a loud voice. The barber's German accent prevented him from pronouncing his name correctly.

"Sir, I believe you're mistaken," Pinkerton replied.

As the barber insisted he was right, Pinkerton angrily denied he was "Mr. Binkerton." As the two men argued, a crowd began to gather. Pinkerton knew that if he was identified as a detective, he would be lynched on the spot. Pinkerton leapt out of his chair and threatened to beat the barber if he continued to insist that he was "Mr. Binkerton."

Intimidated by Pinkerton's fierce attack, the barber reluctantly backed down. Pinkerton then turned to the crowd, apologized for the fuss, and offered to buy everyone a drink in the hotel's bar. His generous invitation was gladly accepted by all. After everyone had drunk enough to think that "Mr. Allen" was the best fellow on earth, Pinkerton excused himself and beat a hasty retreat out of the hotel and headed back to the safety of the North.

The information that Pinkerton and his men gathered enabled McClellan to win several minor battles in the Ohio Valley when war broke out. But in July 1861, Pinkerton received news of a great military disaster. The Northern Army of the Potomac

Lincoln pays a visit to the Pinkerton camp.

had been severely defeated at a little creek called Bull Run in the first major battle of the Civil War.

A good deal of credit for the Southern victory belonged to one of the South's most effective and dedicated spies, Rose O'Neal Greenhow, "the Southern Rose." An extraordinary woman, she became one of Pinkerton's most challenging and intriguing opponents.

Rose O'Neal Greenhow was passionately devoted to the South. She was born and raised in Maryland and grew up in Washington, D.C. where she met and married Dr. Robert Greenhow, a distinguished and cultured physician. Rose was tall and striking looking, with dark hair and dark eyes. She was extremely articulate and well educated. Her combination of beauty, charm and intelligence made her one of the most popular and influential people in Washington.

By the time of the Civil War, Rose O'Neal Greenhow knew everybody in the Capital city worth knowing. She was friendly with the most powerful Northern and Southern politicians in Washington and, after her husband died, close friends with President James Buchanan. Buchanan was a bachelor and his relationship with Rose Greenhow caused many people to gossip about them. Whatever their relationship was, it gave her access to important government secrets. Even before the Civil War, Rose Greenhow obtained secret information for the south about Cuba and Mexico, territories many Southerners wanted to invade in order to expand the slave trade.

After the South seceded from the Union, many Southerners returned home, but Rose Greenhow remained in Washington. She publicly proclaimed her support of the South and her contempt of Lincoln. Because she was so outspoken, many people felt she could not be a spy. But she was actually the queen of the spies. She had been recruited to supply information to the South by Colonel Thomas Jordan, a West Point officer, who gave up his command to join the Southern army. Before leaving Washington, Jordan set up a network of spies and couriers that included government clerks, army officers, architects, doctors, lawyers, cooks, servants, and many Southern women.

In July 1861, as Pinkerton was in Cincinnati gathering military information for General McClellan, it became clear that a major battle was about to take place outside of Washington. The North was so confident of success that a number of prominent citizens and politicians from Washington took champagne, picnic baskets, and opera glasses to the battlefield to watch the fighting.

However, several days before the battle, an attractive young woman by the name of Betty Duvall, dressed like a farm girl, received permission to leave Washington to visit her relatives in the South. She easily passed through Northern lines until she reached the headquarters of the Southern army in Virginia. There she undid her long, beautiful hair letting it fall down her back. She was not showing off her beauty, but uncovering a package that had been concealed in her hairdo, containing military information gathered by Rose Greenhow. Inside were the battle plans of the North. The attack would be lead by General George McDowell, who, with fifty-thousand troops, was ordered to capture the railroad junction at Manassas, twenty-five miles southwest of Washington. From there, McDowell planned to march down to Richmond and crush the rebellion. With that information, the South crushed the North when their armies met. The Union soldiers fled in total panic back to Washington, arriving slightly behind the terrified picnickers.

Southern leaders later publicly acknowledged that it was Rose Greenhow's information that enabled them to win. After the battle General Beauregard, the Southern commander at Bull Run, sent her a note thanking her: "We rely on you for further information. The Confederacy is in your debt." Rose was so effective that a Union General later complained, "she knows my plans better than Lincoln or the cabinet and has four times compelled me to change them." But the victory also contained the seeds of her destruction. After the battle, Lincoln appointed George McClellan in charge of the Army of the Potomac. Accompanying McClellan was Allan Pinkerton, who finally had his chance to organize America's first secret service.

Pinkerton quickly realized that his first task would be to arrest Rose Greenhow. But because of her powerful connections, he needed solid evidence to prove that she was a spy. Pinkerton decided to follow her day and night, hoping that by putting pressure on her, she would make a mistake. Wherever she went, so did his agents. Whenever she was at home, Pinkerton stationed himself and several of his agents outside her house.

If Rose Greenhow was concerned about Pinkerton's surveillance, she did not show it. She was resourceful enough to continue to obtain important information and send it to the South. She thought herself too clever to get caught and believed that, even if she were arrested, she had enough influence to get released.

One stormy winter's night, as the rain poured down hour after hour, Pinkerton and one of his agents stood soaked and shivering outside Rose Greenhow's house. Though it seemed unlikely that anyone would bother to visit Rose on a night like this, Pinkerton was not taking any chances. At the same time, a young Union army captain also thought no one would be foolish enough to watch Rose Greenhow's house on such a miserable night. The captain, who was having a love affair with her, was also supplying her with vital military information. Wanting to bring her a "present," a map showing all the fortified gun ports protecting Washington, he braved the storm and visited her.

Pinkerton watched the captain enter the house, but he could not see what was going on inside. The shutters on the ground floor were closed and he would need a ladder in order to look into the downstairs room from one of the upper windows. Ever resourceful, Pinkerton took off his shoes and stood on his agent's shoulders. As the rain poured down on them he peered into the window and saw Rose Greenhow and her lover analyzing the plans he had brought.

As Pinkerton watched, the two disappeared together into another room. When they returned an hour later, the captain prepared to leave. Pinkerton wrote in his report that as they parted, "I heard the sound of a kiss."

With the rain pouring on his bare head and shoulders and still in stocking feet, Pinkerton followed the captain. When he spotted Pinkerton behind him, he ran into his barracks and ordered his guards to arrest Pinkerton as a criminal. Muddy, shoeless and drenched, Pinkerton certainly looked like one. Not wanting to reveal his identity, Pinkerton refused to give his name. However, he was able to bribe a guard to carry a message to General Thomas Scott, Pinkerton's supervisor. The following day, General Scott brought Pinkerton and the captain to his office. Pinkerton asked the captain if he had ever passed information to anyone that might have given aid and comfort to the enemy. The captain realized he was found out. Pinkerton searched his room and found more incriminating evidence. He was arrested and sent to prison, where he later committed suicide.

Pinkerton felt he needed more evidence against Rose Greenhow before he could send her to jail. He was able to put her under house arrest, hoping that she would eventually confess. But Rose delighted in tormenting her captors in every way she could. She insulted them, threatened to kill them and even managed to destroy some of the evidence that could be used against her.

Pinkerton and his men found many military plans that she had obtained to send to the South. She had gathered all sorts of information including blueprints of fortifications and the number and morale of troops guarding Washington. She had even planned for Southern women to mount the fortifications, spike the Union guns, and give a signal for Southern troops to enter the city. There was also evidence she tried to persuade officers to desert the Union army and go over to the Confederate side.

Most astonishing was her network of spies. They ranged from respectable and seemingly patriotic ladies to bankers, government clerks, lawyers, and other officials. Pinkerton also found a book in which Rose Greenhow had listed the names of all her couriers and how they transmitted their information. They carried messages in all sorts of odd devices from hollow plugs of tobacco to beards and long hair. A cane might have a false top, a trunk a secret compartment, or a hat a hidden lining.

Finally, at Pinkerton's insistence, Rose and her eight-year-old daughter Rose Jr. were taken to prison. The event was more like a ceremony of honor than an arrest. Hundreds of people gathered outside her home, and small boys and men perched on lampposts and in trees waiting for her to appear. When she and her daughter stepped out of their house under police escort, the crowd cheered as if she were a visiting queen rather than a prisoner of the government.

But prison was not enough to stop Rose O'Neal Greenhow from working for her beloved South. Once inside, she held court, receiving all sorts of visitors, including some very influential politicians. She was still able to smuggle important information South, including a letter she wrote to a Virginia newspaper strongly criticizing Pinkerton and Lincoln. She was determined to make a fool of Pinkerton and mobilize public opinion against him. She claimed that she was ill-treated in prison and insisted that she should be treated as a guest of the jail rather than as a prisoner. She had a wonderful flair for the theatrical and she drove Pinkerton crazy, but she had met her match in this grim, determined man. Although many influential people tried to have Rose released and sent back South, Pinkerton refused. He was determined that she be punished for her treason. It was only when her health and that of her daughter were beginning to seriously suffer that Pinkerton withdrew his opposition. Rose was released and allowed to return to Richmond. She was given a hero's welcome and immediately volunteered to travel abroad to raise money and military assistance for the South. She went to France and England and received sympathy and some money, but no promises of military support.

As Rose was returning home her ship was chased by a Northern gunboat as it tried to run past a blockade. The ship escaped but ran aground on a sand bar off the coast of Virginia. Rose, fearing capture, tried to flee to the nearby shore in a small boat despite warnings against doing so by the ship's captain. But

Rose was not a person who took advice easily. Before she could start out, a huge wave capsized her tiny boat and Rose, loaded down with gold she had received in Europe, was swept overboard and drowned.

After Rose Greenhow had been expelled from Washington, Pinkerton concentrated on sending his agents into the South. He even used his own sons as agents on occasion. He would send fourteen-year-old Robert in an air balloon with two other agents to locate and count enemy troops. His oldest son, William, who was sixteen, would dress as a Confederate soldier and slip behind enemy lines with messages for Pinkerton's agents. He traveled barefooted, carrying secret messages written on thin strips of paper between his toes. Robert was instructed that if he was in danger of being caught, he was to pretend he was very shy and rub his feet together in order to destroy the messages.

Pinkerton used his sons because both boys were consumed with war fever and Pinkerton and his wife were afraid that the boys would run off and join the army. He felt that it was safer to have them spy under his command than to fight in the front lines of a regiment.

Though Pinkerton had no equal when it came to uncovering spies, he was almost incompetent when it came to military intelligence. McClellan was reluctant to fight unless he was sure that he had more troops than his opponent. But Pinkerton often overestimated the strength of the enemy. As a result, McClellan sometimes did not attack when he should have and lost opportunities to win victories, and to end the war early. At last, Lincoln, who needed a fighting general, replaced him. Pinkerton, who allowed his friendship for McClellan to cloud his better judgement, was outraged. Pinkerton's loyalty lead him to support

William Pinkerton, age 16, as a Union spy in a rebel uniform.

McClellan, even when it was against his principles. Pinkerton advocated freeing slaves, which McClellan opposed. Yet Pinkerton did not protest when McClellan tried to impose his prejudices against blacks on his troops.

When McClellan was removed from his command by Lincoln, he decided to run for the presidency on the Democratic ticket in the next election. Pinkerton quit his job as head of the secret service and military intelligence, even though Lincoln wanted him to stay. He decided to support McClellan's bid for the presidency. At first, it seemed that McClellan would win easily, as the war was dragging on and the people had become extremely dissatisfied with Lincoln. But then General William Tecumseh Sherman captured Atlanta, Georgia, and the nation overwhelmingly re-elected Lincoln.

Even though Pinkerton was no longer with the secret service, he continued to serve his country by investigating merchants cheating the government by selling shoddy goods to the military. Pinkerton arrested many of them and sent them to jail. When the war ended, Pinkerton returned to Chicago to concentrate on building up his business.

On April 14, 1865, Lincoln was assassinated. Although Pinkerton had been deeply critical of Lincoln over the years, he broke down and wept when he heard the news. "If only I had been there," he told his children, "it wouldn't have happened." Later, his sons remembered that whenever their father spoke about Lincoln, tears would come to his eyes.

8

The Way of the Transgressor Is Hard: Admission Twenty-Five Cents

The end of the Civil War did not bring peace to America. There were outbursts of violence throughout the country. In the North, workers began to organize against owners. In the South, returning confederate soldiers began to harass and attack freed blacks. In the West, it was the era of the outlaw. Jesse and Frank James, the Younger, Reno and Dalton brothers, Sam Bass and Belle Star were riding into history. And riding after them in pursuit were Pinkerton agents.

On October 6, 1866, the first train robbery took place. It was the first time that outlaws intercepted a train on route, robbed it, and rode off. Three masked men, John and Simeon Reno and Franklin Sparks, boarded a Ohio and Mississippi train after it left the town of Seymour, Indiana. Knocking the guard unconscious, the trio pushed two safes containing a total of $45,000 out of the moving train and escaped.

Allan Pinkerton was immediately sent for. It was easy for him to establish who committed the crime for the Reno brothers controlled the town of Seymour and nothing happened in their territory without their approval.

Pinkerton recruited a number of people in and around Seymour to spy on the Renos. One of Pinkerton's best agents was Dick Winscott, a bartender in a saloon where the Renos and their gang went to drink, gamble and visit the ladies. One evening, when John Reno, the gang leader, and Franklin Sparks, were drinking in Winscott's saloon, the bartender talked them into having their picture taken by a photographer who just happened to walk in. Reno and Sparks agreed. The photographer was a Pinkerton agent and the photographs were sent directly to Allan Pinkerton's office.

After the Renos' successful robbery of the train, others began to imitate them. Two young outlaws, however, made the mistake of holding up a train in the Renos's territory. Infuriated, the brothers rode out after the two men as if they were a sheriff's posse rather than a gang of outlaws. They caught the two robbers, beat and robbed them of the money they had stolen and then turned them over to a local sheriff!

When the Reno gang struck again, Allan Pinkerton decided he had enough evidence to make his move. Because the Reno brothers were well protected in Seymour, Pinkerton decided not to risk a direct confrontation. He decided to kidnap John Reno,

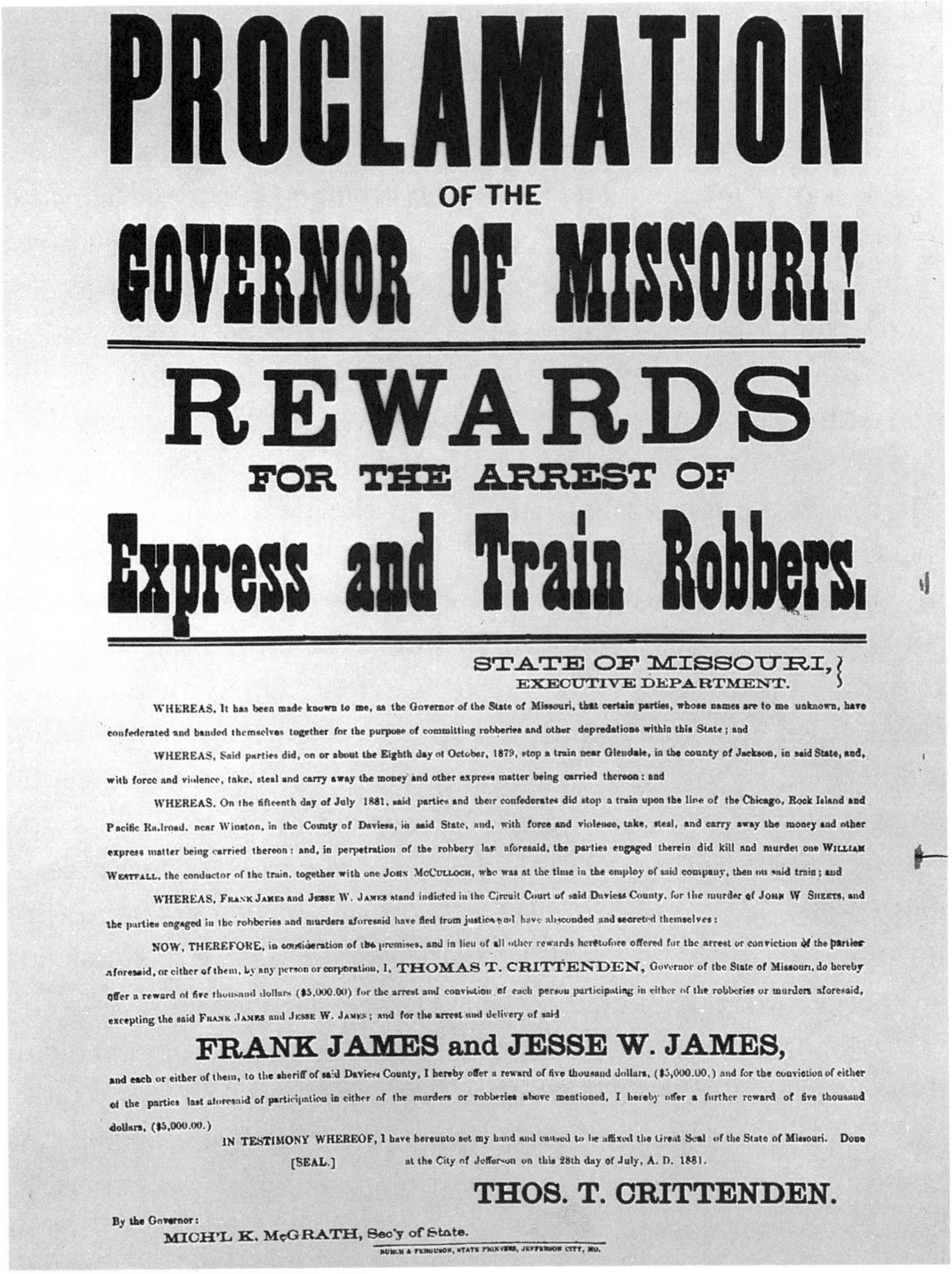

PROCLAMATION

OF THE

GOVERNOR OF MISSOURI!

REWARDS

FOR THE ARREST OF

Express and Train Robbers.

STATE OF MISSOURI,
EXECUTIVE DEPARTMENT.

WHEREAS, It has been made known to me, as the Governor of the State of Missouri, that certain parties, whose names are to me unknown, have confederated and banded themselves together for the purpose of committing robberies and other depredations within this State; and

WHEREAS, Said parties did, on or about the Eighth day of October, 1879, stop a train near Glendale, in the county of Jackson, in said State, and, with force and violence, take, steal and carry away the money and other express matter being carried thereon: and

WHEREAS, On the fifteenth day of July 1881, said parties and their confederates did stop a train upon the line of the Chicago, Rock Island and Pacific Railroad, near Winston, in the County of Daviess, in said State, and, with force and violence, take, steal, and carry away the money and other express matter being carried thereon: and, in perpetration of the robbery las aforesaid, the parties engaged therein did kill and murdet one WILLIAM WESTFALL, the conductor of the train, together with one JOHN McCULLOCH, who was at the time in the employ of said company, then on said train; and

WHEREAS, FRANK JAMES and JESSE W. JAMES stand indicted in the Circuit Court of said Daviess County, for the murder of JOHN W SHEETS, and the parties engaged in the robberies and murders aforesaid have fled from justice and have absconded and secreted themselves:

NOW, THEREFORE, in consideration of the premises, and in lieu of all other rewards heretofore offered for the arrest or conviction of the parties aforesaid, or either of them, by any person or corporation, I, THOMAS T. CRITTENDEN, Governor of the State of Missouri, do hereby offer a reward of five thousand dollars ($5,000.00) for the arrest and conviction of each person participating in either of the robberies or murders aforesaid, excepting the said FRANK JAMES and JESSE W. JAMES; and for the arrest and delivery of said

FRANK JAMES and JESSE W. JAMES,

and each or either of them, to the sheriff of said Daviess County, I hereby offer a reward of five thousand dollars, ($5,000.00,) and for the conviction of either of the parties last aforesaid of participation in either of the murders or robberies above mentioned, I hereby offer a further reward of five thousand dollars, ($5,000.00.)

IN TESTIMONY WHEREOF, I have hereunto set my hand and caused to be affixed the Great Seal of the State of Missouri. Done

[SEAL.] at the City of Jefferson on this 28th day of July, A. D. 1881.

THOS. T. CRITTENDEN.

By the Governor:
MICH'L K. McGRATH, Sec'y of State.

An 1881 wanted poster for Frank and Jesse James.

jail him in another town and arrange for a speedy trial. Pinkerton did not concern himself with the subtleties of the law. He firmly believed the ends justified the means and whenever he felt handicapped by the law, he was willing to bend it in his favor.

To carry out his plan, Pinkerton arranged for a special train to arrive in Seymour a few minutes before the regularly scheduled express. He knew that the local people liked to gather at the train station to watch the express pass by. Winscott persuaded John Reno to accompany him without his bodyguards to the station to watch the train as it passed. Reno agreed, feeling that nobody would try to capture him in public. As the two men were talking, Pinkerton's train came round the bend and stopped at the station. Six men jumped off and, recognizing John Reno from his picture, caught the outlaw completely off-guard. Before he could draw his guns, they carried him screaming and kicking to their train as an astonished crowd watched. Once on board the train, Reno was roped and handcuffed. He was quickly tried, found guilty, and sentenced to prison. In his autobiography written some years later, he vividly recalled his entrance into the Indiana penitentiary, "When we arrived at the prison gate, I looked up and read in large letters over the entrance: 'the way of the transgressor is hard; admission twenty-five cents.' But I was on the deadhead list and went in free."

With the leader of the gang in jail, Allan sent his son William to track down the three remaining Reno brothers William, Frank, and Simeon and the rest of the gang. The young Pinkerton was now twenty-two-years-old and as strong, tough and stubborn as his father. He learned that the gang had committed a series of holdups and patiently he began to track them down. As his father had taught him, William interviewed hundreds of people for

Yours Truly
W. A. Pinkerton
1876

William Pinkerton

Robert Pinkerton

information. He pieced together little bits and scraps that he had learned until finally he located a saloon which some of the gang members frequented. For several days and nights he staked out the bar, hoping the gang might show up. While none did, William noticed that a wealthy and prominent local citizen by the name of Michael Rogers visited the bar regularly. William wondered why a man of Roger's means would drink in such a disreputable place. Checking on Rogers background, Pinkerton discovered that this seemingly solid citizen had a police record. William decided to stake out Roger's house. One morning just before dawn, Frank Reno and two other gang members slipped into Roger's home. Immediately the detectives broke in and arrested everyone. Frank Reno protested his innocence and threatened to sue William Pinkerton for false arrest. William searched the house but found no evidence of a crime. Just as he was about to leave, Pinkerton noticed smoke coming from the stove. Opening it, he found eleven thousand dollars in cash that was about to go up in flames. The four men were arrested, but the following day, April 1, 1868, they broke out of jail, painting a message for William Pinkerton on the jailhouse wall: APRIL FOOL.

One month later, the Reno gang robbed another train outside of Seymour. The train's engineer and the messenger guarding the safe were beaten unconscious and the conductor was shot down when he opened fire on the outlaws. The gang rode off with $96,000 and immediately split up. Some fled to Illinois and others crossed to Canada.

William Pinkerton first tracked the three outlaws who had fled to Illinois and captured them without difficulty. He instructed six of his men to take them to jail in Indianapolis. To get there, they had to take a train to Seymour and then change for the Indianapolis express. As the Pinkerton agents rode to Seymour with their prisoners, their train mysteriously stopped every ten or fifteen minutes, waited for awhile, and then started again. The conductor explained that the stops were for routine maintenance, but the detectives nervously wondered whether someone was going to attempt to rescue their prisoners. Nothing happened, but when the train finally arrived in Seymour, the connecting train to Indianapolis had long departed.

The Pinkerton agents decided that it was unwise to keep the gang locked up in a town where the gang members had many friends—and enemies. With the help of the local sheriff; they put their prisoners in a wagon and set out for a nearby town. But a few miles outside of Seymour, they were suddenly confronted by a mob of two-hundred masked riders. The leader ordered the Pinkerton guards to return to town. Then the masked riders grabbed the prisoners and, taking them to the nearest tree, promptly hung all three of them.

Shortly afterwards a Pinkerton agent arrested William and Simeon Reno along with several other gang members and took them to the town of Lexington, Indiana, for trial. Hundreds of vigilantes gathered to lynch the prisoners and the governor was forced to call out the militia. The Reno brothers and other gang members were transferred to another jail for safety. They were kept there until Allan Pinkerton could bring back the last gang members who had fled to Canada.

Allan Pinkerton located Frank Reno and the rest of the outlaws outside of Windsor, Canada, and arrested them. But the Canadians objected to Pinkerton's failure to follow proper procedures and refused to extradite them. The United States government began to negotiate with Canada for the return of the outlaws as Pinkerton impatiently waited. As the two countries argued, Pinkerton traveled back and forth between Detroit and Windsor on a ferry. On one such trip, as Pinkerton started to board, he heard a click directly behind him. His instinct told him someone was cocking a revolver at his head. Whirling around, he caught the gunman's hand and put his finger in the trigger guard so the gun could not be fired. He wrestled the gun away from his would-be killer, and after a brief, violent fight, he subdued him. The gunman's name was Dick Barry. He was a well-known criminal from Detroit and claimed that he had been hired by William Wood, the head of the American Secret Service to assassinate Pinkerton. The charge was vigorously denied and never proved, but there were rumors that Wood might have been connected with the Renos. Two days later another gunman in Detroit shot at Pinkerton, but missed. Pinkerton ran him down and arrested him, but the police let him escape. Whoever was plotting against Pinkerton had good political connections.

Finally Canada agreed to extradite the last members of the Reno gang on the condition that they would be protected from a lynch mob. The United States agreed. When the outlaws were returned to Indiana, vigilantes demanded they be hung while the Renos's supporters threatened to kill anyone who tried to do so. After awhile, the tension died down and the governor sent the militia home. It seemed that the Reno gang would stand trial after all.

On December 7, the engineer who had been severely beaten by the Renos during their train robbery died from his wounds. An unnatural quiet settled over the town. At midnight of December 12, as Christmas neared, an unscheduled train slipped into the station and a large group of masked men quickly moved into the town. Anyone they met was held captive at gunpoint. They cut the telegraph wires and then went to sheriff Thomas Lovelace's house for his keys to the jail. Lovelace protested and was shot in the arm.

The group then went to the jail and warned the two deputies inside that unless they opened the door, they would be hung with the Renos. The deputies yielded and the vigilantes entered. Holding their torches high, the mob searched the cells for the Renos and the rest of the gang, while the other prisoners crouched in fear. The outlaws were dragged to the upper tier of the jail where ropes were thrown around the rafters and the nooses placed around their necks. One by one, the men were thrown off the upper level. But their necks did not break and they slowly strangled. When one gang member, Charlie Anderson, was thrown off the tier, the noose slipped from his neck and he crashed to the floor below. Screaming for mercy, he was dragged upstairs and hung again. This time, they let him down easy so the noose wouldn't slip. Simeon was also hung in the same way, but after the vigilantes left, he regained consciousness. As the other prisoners in the jail watched in horror from their locked cells, Simeon desperately tried to free himself. But his feet just missed touching the floor by inches and for thirty minutes, he hung in the air, struggling frantically as the life was strangled from him.

The next day the shocked community gathered to see the bodies of the Reno gang, and others, swinging from the jailhouse rafters. Shortly afterward, warning notices were publicly posted warning the Reno's friends to leave town or share their fate.

The Reno case was the last time Allan Pinkerton would ride after outlaws in the West. His sons William and Robert now took his place as they chased the most famous outlaws in nineteenth century America—the James-Younger gangs.

Frank and Jesse James and Cole Younger and his three brothers were all Confederate veterans. During the Civil War, they had ridden with Quantrill's raiders, a band of Southern guerillas which terrorized Kansas and Missouri, massacring soldiers and civilians alike. The two groups of brothers had joined forces after the war and raided the banks of Missouri, killing several people.

Allan Pinkerton's agency was asked to track the gang in 1871, but had to call off its investigation. One of the country's worst depressions had occurred and the agency was in serious financial trouble—Allan Pinkerton constantly complained about money in his letters. There was a danger that he might have to close his business. But prosperity returned and in 1874, the Pinkertons resumed their chase of the James-Younger Gang.

At first, Pinkerton reluctantly sent a young agent named John Whicher to Missouri. Whicher had pleaded with Pinkerton for the assignment and Allan, against his better judgment, let him go. Whicher's body was found riddled with bullets alongside a road. Shortly afterward, two men hired by the agency, Louis Lull and John Boyle, both former policemen and Ed Daniels, a deputy sheriff, began to search the back country for the Younger brothers. Unfortunately they found them. Lull described the meeting—before he died from John Younger's bullet wounds. He said that he and the other two detectives met two men on horseback, one armed with a double-barreled shotgun, the other with two revolvers. They were John and Jim Younger. Boyle suddenly bolted and rode off, leaving Lull and Daniels to face the Youngers. Lull drew his pistol and fatally wounded John Younger.

With superhuman strength Younger fired his shotgun, killing Daniels and then rode after the fleeing Lull. Younger ran him down, fired his shotgun at him point blank, then collapsed and died. Lull survived for three days before dying from his wounds. Jim Younger collected all their guns to bring back to the gang and then escaped.

Several months later, the police learned that Frank and Jesse James were hiding at their mother's house. The local sheriff and his deputies, led by two unidentified men, believed to be William Pinkerton and one of his agents, surrounded the house. Unknown to them, the James brothers had left, leaving behind Jesse's mother, Zerelda, a Dr. Samuels who was a friend of the family and Jesse's two small half-brothers. The two detectives crept up to the house to see what was going on. When they were spotted, they tossed a flare into the house, hoping it would drive everyone out into the arms of the waiting posse. Unfortunately, the doctor pushed the flare into the fireplace where it exploded, injuring eight-year-old Archie and shredding the arm of Jesse's mother. Archie died several days later and Jesse's mother lost her arm.

The press ripped the Pinkertons for their participation in the raid and local authorities in Missouri were so enraged that they put out murder indictments against them. Allan Pinkerton found himself in the curious position of denying that the agency was involved while at the same time defending what had happened. Jesse swore to kill William and it was rumored that he had gone to Chicago for that purpose. The Pinkertons were never again involved in the James case and it was one of their most notable failures. For eight more years the James and the Younger brothers terrorized the Midwest until finally the Youngers were captured and Jesse James was shot in the back by a former outlaw friend,

Bob Ford. Frank James turned himself in and was granted a pardon.

But as long as the outlaws rode in the Old West, Pinkerton agents pursued them. And like the Jameses and Youngers and Renos, the Pinkertons also became part of the legend of the Old West.

9

It Must Be Death

———— 👁 ————

By 1870, Allan Pinkerton had become a master detective. Not only did he solve crimes that had already been committed, he sometimes was able to sense a crime before it actually happened.

One day, as Pinkerton was walking home from his office, he passed by a man who aroused his suspicions. He had never seen the man before, nor was there anything unusual about him. The man was well dressed, distinguished looking and gave the impression of being a person of leisure.

Yet, there was something about the man that attracted Pinkerton's attention. Although it was nothing more than a feeling, Pinkerton decided to trust his intuition and follow the man.

As the man casually strolled through Chicago, Pinkerton became concerned that the suspect might sense he was being followed. Passing by a clothing store Pinkerton dashed inside and quickly exchanged his hat and coat for a new one and continued to follow the man in his new disguise.

Eventually, the well-dressed man entered a hotel. Pinkerton checked the hotel register and discovered the man's name was John Harmond. When he entered the hotel, Pinkerton had noticed that the street in front had been torn up and was being rebuilt. After making sure that Harmond was in his room for the night, Pinkerton went home where he put on dirty, tattered pants, an old shirt, and ragged shoes and transformed himself into a bricklayer. Just before sunrise he stationed himself in front of the hotel and pretended he was part of the crew fixing the street.

Pinkerton in disguise as a bricklayer.

The next day John Harmond left his hotel and walked to the railroad station where he bought a ticket for Detroit. He then strolled down to the shores of Lake Michigan, unaware that a "bricklayer" was also walking in the same direction. Pinkerton saw Harmond kneel by the water's edge, take a box out of the ground, and, after making sure nobody was around, stuff things in his pocket. To Pinkerton it looked like jewelry and watches, but he couldn't be sure from where he was standing. Harmond then boarded a train for Detroit that was about to depart. Pinkerton knew he had to act immediately. Taking out a pair of handcuffs, he came up behind Harmond, put his arm around his neck and grabbed him. "You're under arrest," he cried out. Harmond began to shout that he was being robbed. The passengers and the conductor ran to his aid, as Harmond appeared to be a gentleman and the roughly-dressed Pinkerton a crook. Fortunately, Pinkerton knew the conductor of the train and identified himself. He handcuffed Harmond, emptied his pockets, and found a load of jewelry, watches and wallets. He took his prisoner to the police station and then, without changing his clothes, returned to the hotel.

The place was in an uproar. Every guest was complaining he had been robbed and the manager was in a panic. Pinkerton banged the front desk with his fist, then leaped on the counter. The manager and the doorman tried to throw Pinkerton out because they thought he was a workman who didn't belong in the hotel. But Pinkerton told the guests that if they wanted their possessions back, they should go to the police station. When nobody believed him, he realized his little masquerade had gone too far, and revealed himself.

Pleased that his disguise fooled even people who knew him well, Pinkerton decided to play a joke on his wife and children. He went home and knocked on the door. When his wife answered, he pretended to be an Irish laborer seeking work. She replied that he should seek the shower instead, wash himself, and get rid of his dirty clothes. Before he could reply, his children called out "Hi Daddy." They had immediately seen through his disguise.

The more successful the agency became, the less time Pinkerton had to handle cases himself. He had to administer his business, especially during the depression years when it was in financial trouble. He had trained his agents extremely well and had complete confidence in their abilities. Kate Warne remained one of his favorite detectives and whenever an opportunity came for them to work together, Pinkerton was delighted.

One day, a man walked into his office with a strange story to tell. He was Captain Charles Sumner, a sea captain who had come to see Pinkerton about his sister Annie Thayer. Although a married woman, she had become romantically involved with a married man by the name of Alonzo Pattmore, a well known politician in Chicago. Pattmore's wife was also living with him, but was very ill and under the care of a nurse. Annie Thayer's husband, Henry, was a sailor far away at sea.

The captain had tried to break up his sister's relationship with Pattmore. She refused, saying that Pattmore intended to marry her, that in fact they had gone through a wedding ceremony, even though the ceremony was invalid. The captain believed Pattmore was a crook and was only interested in inheriting the captain's modest fortune which his sister would inherit. The captain was positive that she had tried to poison him to prevent him from breaking up her involvement with Pattmore.

Pinkerton accepted the case, but before he could begin his investigation, Pattmore's wife died. Suspecting murder, Pinkerton made arrangements with a doctor to perform an autopsy on the dead woman. But Pattmore had cleverly switched the body of his wife with another woman's. Pinkerton located the true grave, but he needed someone willing to break the law and dig up Mrs. Pattmore's body. Pinkerton approached a gravedigger and told him that he needed to examine the body for two good reasons. The first was that he would pay the gravedigger twenty-five dollars. Before Pinkerton could tell the gravedigger the second reason, the man raised his hand: "Stop. Say no more. The first reason is good enough for me." That night Pinkerton and the doctor had their body.

The autopsy showed that Mrs. Pattmore had died of poison as Pinkerton suspected. To crack the case however, they need supporting testimony against Pattmore from Captain Sumner's sister. Pinkerton ordered one of his agents, Mrs. Seaton, to make friends with Mrs. Thayer. She was now living alone in Chicago, waiting to be joined by Pattmore. Although Annie Thayer revealed little about herself to Mrs. Seaton, she did admit she was superstituous and believed in fortune tellers.

Pinkerton sent Kate Warne to take a crash course in fortune telling. When she finished, Pinkerton furnished her with a room and told her to dress the part. Kate played the role to perfection. She dressed herself in an exotic manner, took the name of Mrs. Lucille, and decorated her apartment with all sorts of mysterious pictures and signs. Pinkerton briefed her about Annie Thayer's childhood and present circumstances, going into great detail about her relationship with Pattmore and his wife. Now all Pinkerton had to do was to get Annie to visit her.

Pinkerton then instructed Mrs. Seaton to take a walk with Annie Thayer. He arranged for a boy to pass them handing out leaflets announcing a new fortune teller named Mrs. Lucille, who was available for consultations. When Annie Thayer read the leaflet, she decided to visit the fortune teller and walked right into Pinkerton's trap.

Superbly playing her role as a fortune teller, Kate Warne told Mrs. Thayer all the things she had learned about her from the "spirits in the other world." Kate told her things about her childhood, her married life, and her brother. Annie Thayer was astonished and impressed. Then suddenly the fortune teller became extremely agitated, as if something or someone was

Illustration showing Kate Warne as a fortune teller. It is not known how close the illustrator came to portraying Kate's likeness as there are no known photographs of her available.

overwhelming her. "I see another woman!," she cried out "She is your rival. But a dark shadow fades over her. What can this mean! She is fading away! She vanishes! *It must be death!*" Mrs. Thayer screamed and fainted. But her fascination was even greater than her fear.

Several days later, Annie Thayer returned for another visit. This time Mrs. Lucille went into a trance and pretended she could see what had happened to Pattmore's wife. She said she saw Pattmore bringing his wife some "medicine" for her illness. The more medicine he gave her, the sicker his wife became. The fortune teller described how the poor woman looked at her husband with pleading eyes, suspecting the worst, but helpless to stop him. At the end of her trance Kate Warne cried out: "I do not see Mrs. Pattmore. She is murdered!" Mrs. Thayer again collapsed. When she was revived, she begged the fortune teller to advise her what to do to save herself from punishment. Kate told her that a strange man would approach her on the street. "Do not be afraid. He can be trusted," she said. She described the man to Mrs. Thayer and advised her to tell him everything she knew when he spoke to her.

The next day, as Annie Thayer was out walking, a "strange man" approached her just as the fortune teller had predicted. It was Allan Pinkerton who suggested to Mrs. Thayer that they go to his office and talk. Completely under the fortune teller's spell, Annie Thayer meekly agreed. She told him everything. At Pattmore's trial, she was the star witness. Pattmore was convicted and sent to prison and Mrs. Thayer let go. She and her husband reconciled.

Meanwhile, during the investigation, Kate Warne had developed such a reputation as a fortune teller that people lined up outside her office for consultations. She was quite happy to close her fortune telling business and go back to the life of a detective. But her career ended suddenly. She developed a serious illness, most probably cancer, and died on New Year's day in 1868. Pinkerton's affection for Kate was so great he buried her in his family plot.

The death of Kate Warne was only one of several shocks Allan Pinkerton received in the years immediately following the Civil War. In 1869, he suffered a severe stroke, which almost killed him and left him almost completely paralyzed. Pinkerton refused to accept the doctor's verdict that he would never walk and talk again. His iron will, which so often made him abusive to others, served him well in his illness. He painfully forced himself to walk, one step at a time, until he could walk twelve miles a day. Gradually his powers of speech returned. Eventually he was able to return to work, having "beaten the doctors," as he once said.

It was during his illness that Pinkerton built his great summer estate the Larches 80 miles south of Chicago. The larch is a Scottish tree that Allan and Joan loved. He ordered 85,000 of them shipped over from Scotland and when the first batch died of frost on the New York docks, he ordered another 85,000. The 254 acre estate contained trees, flowers, lawns, pastures, live-stock, dogs, and barns. It was a re-creation of the Scottish countryside with a touch of his early days of Dundee thrown in. The only harsh note in this idyllic scene was made by the armed guards that surrounded the house twenty-four hours a day.

At his estate Pinkerton entertained the rich and powerful of America. Commodore Vanderbilt, General Ulysses S. Grant, August Belmont, Supreme Court Chief Justice Salmon Chase,

Allan and Joan Pinkerton

and their families were among his many guests. The detective was far removed from his days as a poor cooper in the slums of Scotland, passionately denouncing rich and powerful men like those he now proudly invited to his home, and for whom he worked. And no assignment would reveal how far he traveled from his origins than the one he handled for railroad tycoon Franklin B. Gowen—the case of the Molly Maguires.

10

It Is No Ordinary Man I Need in This Matter

———— 👁 ————

On a clear, crisp fall day in 1873, a seedy looking tramp wandered into the coal region of eastern Pennsylvania. His clothes dirty and tattered, a stubble of a beard covering his face, and a clay pipe clenched between his teeth, he seemed no different than any of the hundreds of hobos who passed through the coal fields daily in search of work. But this "tramp" was after more than a meal or a job. He was seeking to make contact with a violent, secret organization known as the Molly Maguires. His name was James McParland and he was Allan Pinkerton's ace undercover agent. His assignment was to uncover and destroy the Mollies.

America in the 1870s was a breeding ground for organizations

James McParland, dedicated Pinkerton detective.

like the Molly Maguires. Another civil war was about to begin. The battlefields would be the coal mines, steel mills, and factories of America and the battle between the workers and the owners. It was the age in which the industrialists became the lords of the earth and ruled America with more power than any ancient king. Workers were treated little better than slaves. They were used until they were useless and then discarded. They had no legal rights, no social security, no medical or unemployment insurance, and no unions to protect them.

If working conditions throughout America were hard, they were brutal in the coal mines. Men worked twelve hours a day, six days a week for ten to thirty-five dollars depending upon their job. Miners were paid by the amount of coal they dug, but the coal was weighed on company scales rigged in favor of the mine owners. Workers were paid in script, money printed by the company, rather than in United States currency. The script could be used only in company-owned stores which charged higher prices than regular stores and which the miners contemptously called gyp-me or pluck-me stores.

The worst part of the job was the dangerous conditions in the mines. Men were frequently killed or maimed by falling rock, dynamite, gas explosions, and poison gases that lay hidden in the mines. During the 1870s, an average of a hundred men were killed each year and three times as many maimed. In one mine disaster in 1871, one hundred and eleven miners died, seventeen of them under the age of fourteen. Those who escaped violent deaths inside the mines usually died agonizing deaths from the dreaded "black lung disease," which most miners catch from inhaling fine particles of coal dust. This disease is a result of poor ventilation inside the mine and once it attacks the lungs, there is no cure.

Many of the men who worked in the mines were Irish immigrants who had come to America to escape the harsh oppression of English rule. Because many were poor, uneducated, and drank heavily they were severely discriminated against. People expressed their hostility openly. "No Irish need apply" was a postscript commonly added to advertisements for jobs or rooms. The Irish in the mines were often the last to be hired and the first to be fired.

In the 1860s a small group of Irish workers formed an American chapter of a secret society known as the Molly Maguires to protect themselves and gain political power. The Mollies began in Ireland in the 1840s to battle the English landlords who oppressed Irish farmers. In America, they attacked not only those who oppressed them, but anyone with whom they had a quarrel. If a Molly was dismissed from a job, beaten in a fight, insulted or injured, the organization sought revenge. Superintendents and foremen were killed, men brutally beaten, buildings dynamited or burned and railroad cars overturned because some member of the Mollies had a grievance. To instill terror in their victims, the Mollies would send them "coffin notices," a sketch of a coffin indicating that the receiver could either leave town or be buried in it.

While many mine owners were willing to make some accommodations to the Mollies, Franklin B. Gowen, president of the Pennsylvania and Reading Coal and Iron Company was not. He was determined not only to crush the Mollies, but any organization of working men that he felt stood in his way. Gowen offered Pinkerton the job, and he accepted without hesitation. The now famous and prosperous detective had put the radical days of his youth far behind him and joined forces with the very sort of men he had once bitterly opposed.

Franklin B. Gowen, who initiated the Mollie Maguire investigations.

Pinkerton quickly decided the only way to put an end to the Mollies was to have an agent infiltrate them and gather evidence to convict them. Pinkerton was too well known to do the job himself. Moreover, his Scots background automatically disqualified him. As he wrote in his account of the case, "It is no ordinary man I need in this matter. He must be an Irishman and a Catholic, as only this class of people can find admission to the Mollie Maguires. My detective should become, to all intensive purposes, one of the order and continue so while he remains in the case before us. He should be hardy, tough and capable of laboring."

Pinkerton interviewed a number of his agents for the job, but none of them seemed right. Then one day, as he was riding a streetcar in Chicago, he noticed that the conductor was one of his agents assigned to catch thieves and pickpockets who worked the line. His name was James McParland. After briefly talking with him, Pinkerton felt that McParland was the man he was looking for. McParland was an Irish immigrant and Roman Catholic, who had worked at a variety of jobs in America before becoming a detective for the agency. Although he was only five feet nine and weighed one hundred forty-five pounds, McParland was tough, fearless and an excellent boxer. He was handy with a gun, could sing and dance, liked to gamble, and was a ladies' man. McParland accepted the assignment. He took the name of James McKenna, and inventing a criminal past for himself as a counterfeiter and a killer, he set out for the coal fields disguised as a tramp.

McParland's first task was to make contact with the Mollies, which was easier said than done. While Mollies were everywhere around him, they were visible nowhere. No one admitted to being a Molly. No one would discuss the subject or dare talk about it with a stranger.

McParland's persistence paid off. He learned that in the town of Pottsville, Pat Dormer, a fierce giant of a man, ran a hotel called the Sheridan House where Mollies gathered to drink and play cards. One night, as the bar was packed and the liquor flowed freely, McParland approached the hotel. Inside, he could hear the sound of a fiddle playing. Putting one hand on the doorknob, he took a deep breath, pushed the door open and entered. Every eye in the place turned toward him. Pretending to be drunk, McParland began to dance a jig in time to the music. As his dancing became wilder, the men in the bar clapped their hands to encourage him. And when McParland concluded his entertainment by singing a beautiful Irish ballad praising the Molly Maguires in his fine tenor's voice, he won the crowd over.

Pat Dormer himself came over and shook McParland's hand, praised his talent, and invited him to join them in a friendly card game. Seated across the table from McParland was a powerfully built man by the name of Frazier. After several minutes of play, McParland shot out of his seat and seizing Frazier by the wrist, accused him of cheating. He forced Frazier to reveal that he had dealt himself six cards instead of five. Immediately Frazier cursed McParland and challenged him to a fight. Everyone waited to see what McParland would do.

Without hesitation, McParland removed his jacket and the two men hammered away at each other on the barroom floor as the crown cheered them on. Although Frazier was almost twice McParland's size, the smaller man outfought him. He landed blow after blow on Frazier's face until the man was so battered and bloody, he couldn't fight any more. To show there was no hard feelings, McParland then bought him a drink as the crowd gathered around him and patted his back for entertaining them with such "a grand fight." Dormer was very impressed by McParland's fighting ability and courage. McParland took Dormer into his confidence and told him that his name was James McKenna and that he was a counterfeiter and murderer on the run. He also told Dormer that in Ireland he had once been a member of the Ancient Order of Hibernians, a secret society connected to the Molly Maguires. "But that was a long time ago," he said, then added he remembered nothing of it. He also confided in Dormer that he had a little of the counterfeit "goods" on him which he passed from time to time when he needed money. But he would soon need work and he asked Dormer to help find him a job.

With a letter of recommendation from Dormer, McParland contacted a number of Molly leaders as he looked for a job. In the town of Shenandoah, he met Muff Lawler, who rented him a room. In nearby Girardsville, McParland introduced himself to Jack Kehoe, a man whom many regarded as the most dangerous Molly of them all.

When McParland first visited Kehoe in his saloon, he again charmed everyone with his singing and dancing. But Kehoe was not an easy man to fool. He put McParland to the test by giving him certain secret signs of the Order of the Hibernians. When McParland failed to respond, Kehoe remarked, "I see you know nothing of the present."

"Faith, that's certainly true," McParland replied, "It's a very long time since I was within."

"That shouldn't matter," Kehoe answered, looking squarely at McParland, "for I'm an old-timer too."

McParland knew that if Kehoe even slightly suspected he was an informer, he would be killed immediately. But fortunately a whiskey salesman whom Kehoe knew entered the bar and interrupted them, giving McParland an excuse to leave.

Returning to Shenandoah, McParland began to carry out one of the most difficult parts of his assignment. Pinkerton had insisted that McParland write daily reports on everything he discovered and mail these reports to his Philadelphia office. It was a dangerous requirement, for if anyone even suspected that McParland was writing any letters, his life would be in danger. How was he to carry out such a dangerous assignment? He needed to have a pen, ink, paper and stamps, and he needed to be able to write his reports in a place where no one would see him.

McParland used great ingenuity in carrying out his orders. He made a secret pouch in his boots for stamps, carried a pen point in a box with a number of other odds and ends, and carried writing paper in his carpetbag but left the bag unlocked to avoid inviting curiosity. For ink, he used the liquid blue with which his landlord's wife washed clothes.

Every night, after his roommate fell asleep, McParland would sneak into the kitchen and light a candle. He would write his reports, dipping his steel-tipped pen point in liquid blue. When he finished, he would walk several miles to the post office to mail the letter. If he was caught in the rain or snow, he would make a fire, dry off his clothes before going to bed, and then dispose of the embers in the fireplace so no one would suspect he had been in the kitchen. Sometimes he would fall into bed just as everyone else was waking up.

Muff Lawler, McParland's landlord, finally was able to get the detective a job in the mines. Although McParland had done hard work all his life, nothing he experienced before prepared him for his new job. For twelve hours a day, he shoveled twenty tons of coal into railway cars. By the day's end, his hands were so blistered and bleeding that he could hardly hold a knife and fork. After five days, his hands were mashed by a carload of coal and McParland lost his job. Despite the injury, every night he painfully wrote his reports to Pinkerton.

Even though he made many friends among the Mollies, McParland had not been invited to join the organization. Finally he let it be known that since there was no future for him in the coal regions, he might seek his fortune elsewhere. Lawler told him not to be too hasty. Several weeks later, as McParland was drinking in Lawler's saloon, a group of Mollies entered, had one drink, and went upstairs. Only one of the Mollies and McParland remained. McParland realized he was either going to be invited to join the Mollies or be killed. After a few tense moments, he was invited upstairs and formally sworn in as a member. Kneeling, he took the oath, pledging absolute secrecy about the order. He made the sign of the cross, paid the three dollar membership fee, and drank a toast "to the Emperor of France and Don Carlos of Spain." He was then given the "goods," the secret signs and passwords that enabled Mollies who did not know each other to identify themselves as members. If two men met and one wanted to see if the other belonged to the organization, he would put a fingertip from his right hand into the corner of his right eye. The other would respond by catching the right lapel of his coat with the little finger of his right hand.

If two men got into a quarrel, one would say: "Your temper is high." If the other replied, "I have good reason," the two men would shake hands and buy each other drinks. If two strangers

Here an illustrator showed McParland taking the oath of the Mollie Maguires.

who were Mollies passed each other on a road at night, one would test the other by saying: "The nights are very dark." The other would reply, "They will soon end." These signs and passwords were changed every three months.

McParland became so popular that shortly after he was accepted into the Mollies, his name was proposed as a bodymaster or leader of a local group. Fearing that the job would make him an accessory to any crimes committed, he managed to convince the members to elect his friend Frank McAndrews instead. Since McAndrews couldn't read or write, McParland volunteered to be McAndrew's secretary, which made it easier for him to write and send his reports to Philadelphia.

It did not take long for McParland to find himself in the middle of a murder plot. At a meeting in Jack Kehoe's saloon, Kehoe insisted that the Mollies kill a Welsh night watchman by the name of Gomer James. James had killed a Molly in a quarrel and was a member of a notorious Welsh gang called the Modocs. McParland was in a bind. If he objected too strongly to Gomer's murder, he ran the risk of being expelled. If he went along, he would be an accomplice to murder. The crisis intensified when Kehoe proposed that McParland do the job. To prove that he was not stable enough for that sort of work, McParland drank himself into a stupor for three days. McParland smuggled letters to Franklin Gowen warning him that James was on the Mollies' murder list. The Welsh miner was taken to a hiding place. Kehoe became so enraged when he heard of James escape that he almost beat to death one of his friends for not having carried out his orders to kill James.

Allan Pinkerton knew that his agent was under enormous strain. Several times during the undercover operation, he and McParland had met in Philadelphia. Pinkerton was shocked at the changes in McParland's appearance. He barely recognized him. McParland had become thin, bald, and aged. The heavy drinking, the poverty and his physical injuries had taken their toll. But McParland was in good spirits and vowed to continue until the case was solved.

No sooner had McParland solved one crisis than another appeared. Kehoe had decided to kill a man by the name of Bill "Bully" Thomas who had made the mistake of shooting at a Molly. Even though Thomas had missed, Kehoe decided he was to be punished and ordered McParland and two other Mollies to do the job. But on the day before the killing was to take place,

McParland collapsed with a heavy cold. When the gunmen arrived to pick him up, they saw that he was in no shape to go with them. Not only was McParland unable to do the job, he was also unable to warn the victim. His only hope was that the killers would fail.

The following day, the gunmen returned to McParland's room. He asked if they had missed catching up with Thomas. One grinned and said no, "We surprised him in the stable . . . The fellow was game to the last . . . He had no weapon, but he threw his black hat at me. I fired my gun and he was hit and staggered . . . And then the boys sent two or three more into him and he fell."

Thomas, though severely wounded, survived. But several others marked for death were murdered. Whether the Mollies killed them all as has been charged has been disputed. It was a time when the miners had been on strike for almost six months and tensions were high. The coal companies were evicting families from their homes and company stores were refusing them food, attempting to starve the men into submission. Killings, arson and violence were common. The Mollies did murder several people including Gomer James, who had foolishly returned to the region despite McParland's warnings.

The rash of murders so angered people that action was finally taken against the Mollies. Three men were arrested for one of murders and one of them, James Kerrigan, shocked the organization by agreeing to turn state's evidence against the others.

As Kerrigan identified the killers, Jack Kehoe received a report warning him that McParland was really a Pinkerton detective. There was no proof to back up this charge and only McParland's popularity and reputation as a dangerous man saved him from immediate execution. When Frank McAndrews warned McParland that people were saying he was a detective, McParland immediately went to confront Kehoe.

"What's this I hear yer been saying against me?" McParland demanded to know.

"I have heard told ye are not what you seem, but a detective. I have heard it some time ago, but I didn't believe a word of that yarn," Kehoe replied.

"Well, I want someone to prove it," McParland angrily answered. "Let the order try me. I will stand trial and . . . if I find out who is lying against me, it will go hard with him. I shall kill the scoundrel if I hang for it."

Kehoe seemed impressed with McParland's boldness and promised him a trial. But McParland guessed that Kehoe would not call a trial but have him killed instead. Still, McParland decided to stay and try and bluff his way out of the situation. It was a dangerous game. Everywhere he went, McParland was followed. Whenever McParland met Mollies on the street, they turned away from him. In one saloon he stood up on the counter and called out, "A round for the house. Let's see the man who won't drink with James McKenna." Everyone drank, for no one would dare insult him to his face.

Kehoe met with McAndrews and other bodymasters and pleaded with them to kill McParland "before he hangs half the people in the valley." They agreed. One night assassins waited for him to return home to beat him to death, but McParland changed his route. Another night, a known killer offered to walk beside McParland on a dark street. McParland coolly accepted the gunman's invitation but made the man walk in front of him. Everywhere he turned, he spotted gunmen waiting for the chance to kill him. His few remaining friends could do nothing to help him. Finally, on March 7, 1876, almost three years after he had first entered the coal region, James McParland finally slipped to safety in Philadelphia accompanied by one of Pinkerton's agents. He took with him a tremendous amount of knowledge about the Mollies and their violent ways.

McParland's job was not finished. Gowen wanted him to testify in court against the Mollies. McParland flatly refused. His life would be worthless if he did so. But Gowen kept pressuring him and finally McParland gave in. One month before he was to appear in court, the Pinkertons conducted a series of lightning raids in the coal fields and arrested eleven men including Jack Kehoe, and took the once powerful Molly leaders to jail handcuffed and in chains.

On May 6, 1877, James McParland, fashionably dressed and in high spirits, entered the packed courtroom and began his testimony. Day after day, as the defendants sat shaken and stunned, McParland elaborated in great detail their violent activities. He named specific killers, the time and dates of their crimes, how the plans were made, and who made them. He was a superb prosecution witness, clear and unwavering in his testimony. He supplied details that only an insider could have known. The defense attorneys attacked him, trying to discredit him any way they could. They accused him of complicity in crimes because he failed to warn the victims. McParland answered that he had warned people whenever he could, but not when "I was afraid of being assassinated myself." He stated quite openly, "I would not lose my life for all the men in this courthouse." After McParland testified, other Mollies came out of hiding and offered to exchange information in return for their lives. At a series of subsequent trials, their testimony alone helped convict and condemn other Mollies.

On a beautiful spring day in June of 1877, nineteen young men wearing red roses and carrying crucifixes mounted the gallows. At least one of them was innocent but tragically the jury had not been careful in distinguishing the innocent from the guilty. Ten were hung together, including Jack Kehoe who died a slow, horrible death when the rope around his neck slipped, slowly choking him. Several years later, Franklin Gowen, whose fortunes had suddenly reversed, shot himself in a hotel room in Washington.

After the case was long over, while travelling on an ocean liner sailing from America to England, William Pinkerton fell into conversation with a writer of English mysteries, Sir Arthur Conan Doyle. William told the author the story of the Molly Maguires. The case so impressed him that when Doyle returned home, he used it as the basis for a novel called *The Valley of Fear*. In the novel the great fictional detective Sherlock Holmes vainly tries to save the life of the Pinkerton agent, modeled on James McParland, who testified against the Mollies.

In reality, James McParland had a long career with the Pinkertons. Allan Pinkerton and his agency were praised for his destruction of the Molly Maguires. Yet, many working people regarded the violence of the Mollies as a misguided response to the violence of the coal operators. They saw them as a product of the conditions that existed in the mines, where labor unions were weak and miners had no peaceful way to express their grievances. While many condemned the violence of the Mollies, they also condemned Allan Pinkerton for taking sides with those who were making life unbearable for them.

11

It Had Been My Principle to Use Females for the Detection of Crime

———————— 👁 ————————

After destroying the Molly Maguires, Allan Pinkerton added a new dimension to his detective career. He became a writer of detective stories, or more accurately, he turned over outlines of his cases to professional writers. The 1870s was an era in which the fictional detective hero was quite popular, especially in the dime novels which were the equivalent of today's paperbacks. The stories were written in the overblown, melodramatic style of the day and while sometimes it may be hard to separate fact from fiction, most of Pinkerton's books were based on actual cases. Altogether, eighteen titles were published under Allan Pinkerton's name.

Pinkerton was a stern parent, and as his children were growing up, he kept them under strict control. His daughter Joan, named after her mother, was his favorite. When she was a child, and he was away from home, he would write her and illustrate his letters to her with funny drawings of cats to amuse her. As she grew older, he came to depend upon her more and more. But while she usually obeyed her father's wishes, Joan, like her father, had a strong will of her own. And when she decided to marry a man whom her father opposed, the battle lines were drawn.

When Joan was 22 she met William Chalmers, the brother of one of her friends, and fell in love. He was from a prominent Chicago family and there was no rational reason that Pinkerton could object to his daughter's choice. But Pinkerton was stubborn and overprotective. He insisted that Chalmers wasn't good enough for his daughter. Trying to justify his irrational response, he used phrenological charts to argue that the shape of Chalmer's head, proved him to be "weak-brained." At first his daughter tried to reason with him. She even agreed to travel to Europe for six months to try and forget Chalmers. But when she returned, Joan was all the more determined to marry the man she loved. Pinkerton refused to grant his permission and, acting like a spoiled child, said he and his wife would not attend the wedding if she went through with her plans. One night when Chalmers was visiting Joan at their home, Pinkerton discovered them sitting in the parlor together late at night with the lights out. In melodramatic fashion, he threw Chalmers out of the house and told him never to return. Several days later Joan left home and moved in with her twin brother Robert. Gradually a compromise was worked out and Joan returned home. Her mother was sick and her condition was aggravated by the fighting. Her father gradually accepted his daughter's choice. It turned out to be an excellent marriage for despite Pinkerton's low opinion of his future son-in-law, Chalmers became one of the nation's shrewdest and most successful industrialists.

While Pinkerton was busy trying to deny his daughter her right to chose her own husband, he was, ironically, fighting a battle over women's rights within his own agency. Several Pinkerton branches had refused to hire women detectives and Pinkerton blasted them. He wrote, "It has been my principle to use females for the detection of crime where it has been useful and necessary . . . I can trace it back to the time when I first hired Kate Warne up until the present time. And I still intend to use females whenever it can be done judiciously."

It was becoming clear by now that Pinkerton was under great emotional and physical strain. While he returned to a full schedule of work after his devastating stroke, he was slowly becoming weaker. By 1880, although Allan went to work every day, his two sons William and Robert had taken over. But the transition was not an easy one. Despite his infirmities, Pinkerton was determined to hold on to the company as long as he could. "I mean to be the principal of the firm and will continue to do so until death claims me," he said. There were terrible fights between him and his sons, and in Pinkerton's letters one gets a sense that "Willie," his oldest, was fighting against some kind of illness, perhaps alcoholism. On several occassions, Robert handed in his resignation, usually after a fierce fight with his father. Yet, Allen was not blind to what he was doing to his children. In a moment of unexpected self-awareness he wrote Robert, "My father, I am sure, could be kinder to a son than I have been with you."

WILLIAM A. PINKERTON AND ROBERT A. PINKERTON
World's Premier Detectives sojourning at Hot Springs, Arkansas

As this photo's caption indicates, William and Robert have by now sur-
passed their father's fame as great detectives.

In August of 1882, Allan Pinkerton was invited to be the guest of honor at a reception for John Brown's widow in Chicago's Farweli Hall. For all his worldly success, Allan Pinkerton still cherished those days when he and Brown fought as comrades against slavery. Many who attended the conference reminisced about those days and the great friendship that existed between the two men, and the important role that Pinkerton played in the underground railroad.

Two years later, Pinkerton, confined to a wheelchair, but as stubborn as ever, tried to walk a few steps against doctor's orders and fell. He went into a coma from which he never recovered. On July 1, 1884 he died at the age of sixty-five. Several months later, his wife Joan died. She had told others that after Allan's death life no longer had any meaning for her.

The business was now in the hands of William and Robert Pinkerton. Like their father in many ways, they were stubborn, dogmatic, and honorable. They were also every bit as courageous, pursuing criminals with the same relentless determination. They and their agents solved a number of spectacular crimes. They tracked and arrested Herman Mudgett, known as "America's Bluebeard," who murdered twenty-seven people, most of them women and children. Their agents infiltrated the famous Hole-in-the-Wall gang led by Butch Cassidy and the Sundance Kid and drove them into exile to Bolivia, South America, where they were believed to be killed. A Pinkerton agent, Sam Dimaio, was the first detective to infiltrate the Mafia and gather evidence that led to the conviction imprisonment and hanging, of several of their leaders.

But these spectacular cases were overshadowed to some degree by the Pinkerton agency's role in breaking strikes. After

Allan's death the Pinkerton industrial division, which had been separate from the detective bureaus, provided guards to protect plants, mines, and railroads. Pinkerton agents also infiltrated labor unions to spy on the leadership, despite the fact that Allan Pinkerton had prohibited such activity in his original charter. The Pinkerton police were hated by the unions partially because William Pinkerton insisted that his guards be deputized by local sheriffs so that they could make arrests. Pinkerton agents and strikers clashed throughout the 1880s, but the conflict came to a tragic head during the Homestead Steel strike of 1892.

A bitter strike had broken out at one of the steel plants owned by the industrialists Andrew Carnegie and Henry Frick in Homestead, Pennsylvania. Frick was determined to break the union and refused to negotiate with it in good faith. To protect his property, Frick employed the Pinkerton agency to send three hundred armed watchmen to guard the plant from the strikers. On July 5, the guards came down the Monongahela river by boat and tried to disembark at Homestead. They were greeted by a mob of several thousand angry strikers and their families. Shots rang out and within seconds two guards and several steelworkers were dead and several others injured. Throughout the day, the steelworkers and the guards exchanged fire, but the Pinkerton agents were greatly outnumbered and it was only a matter of time before the strikers would attack them and burn the boat. The leader of the union arranged for a truce and agreed to allow the Pinkerton guards to depart without being harmed as long as they turned in their guns. But while the strike leaders were sincere in their pledge, there were many angry strikers who wanted revenge. As the Pinkerton guards filed past them, they were beaten and two men were killed.

The strike seriously damaged the Pinkerton's reputation. Newspapers and many Congressmen criticized the agency for playing a role in the strike in the first place. Yet, providing plant security had become an important part of the Pinkertons' operation. It was not until Robert Pinkerton II, Allan's great-grandson, headed the agency in the 1930s that the Pinkerton's modified their industrial policy and again prohibited spying against labor unions.

A century and a half has passed since Allan Pinkerton started his detective business with six employees. Today the agency employs over fifty thousand people, most of them as security guards in banks and plants throughout the country. It has become a modern corporation, using the latest technology to prevent crimes rather than solve them. Much of the work the agency used to do is now done by the FBI and local police departments.

Today, Allan Pinkerton is remembered as America's first private detective. He was a legend in his day and gained a national and international reputation for solving difficult crimes. But if he could choose one thing to be remembered for, perhaps it might be those danger-filled nights when he and John Brown rode side by side, ready to lay down their lives for the freedom of their fellow human beings.

For Further Reading

If you are interested in reading more about Allan Pinkerton and the events he participated in, the following books are suggested:

Boyer, Richard. *The Legend of John Brown*. New York: Alfred Knopf, 1973.

Broehl, Wayne J. *The Molly Maguires*. Massachusetts: Cambridge University Press, 1964.

Brooks, Thomas R. *Toil and Trouble, A History of American Labor*. New York: Dell Publishing Company, 1971.

Horan, James B. *The Pinkertons: The Detective Dynasty That Made History*. New York: Bonanza Books, 1967.

Horan, James B. *Desperate Men*. New York: Bonanza Books, 1949.

Nevins, Allan. *Ordeal of the Union*. New York: Charles Scribner's and Sons, 1947.

INDEX

Thayer case, 85–88
Wilmington and Baltimore Railroad case, 46–47

Quantrill's raiders, 79

Reno gang, 69–70, 72, 75–78, 81
    Frank, 72, 75
    John, 70, 72
    Simeon, 70, 72, 76, 78
    William, 72, 76
Roche, Frank, 32
Rogers, Michael, 75

Samuels, Dr., 80
Sanford, Edward S., 31, 32
Saunders, Mr., 25–28
Saunders, Mrs. 25–28
Scott, Thomas, 63
Seaton, Mrs., 86, 87
Secret Service, 77
    Pinkerton and, 2, 44, 47–54
Sparks, Franklin, 70
Star, Belle, 69
Sumner, Charles, 85, 86
Sundance Kid, the, 112

Thayer, Annie, 85–88
Thayer, Henry, 85, 87
Thomas, Bill "Bully," 103–4

Underground railroad, 13–14, 36, 112

Valley of Fear, The, 107
Vanderbilt, Commodore, 89, 91
Vincent, Henry, 7

Warne, Kate, 32, 33, 85–89
    hiring of, 24, 110
Warner, Frank, 25–28
Washburne, 53
Webster, Timothy, 46, 50
Whicher, John, 79
White, John, 32–34
Wilmington and Baltimore Railroad, 46–47
Wilson, John, 43
Winscott, Dick, 70, 72
Wood, William, 77

Younger gang, 69, 79–81
    Cole, 79
    Jim, 79–80
    John, 79–80